VAGUS NERVE BRAIN-BELLY RESET

SOMATIC THERAPY FOR COMPLEX PTSD & GUT HEALTH: 40+BEGINNER EXERCISES FOR OPTIMAL MIND-BODY HEALING

KIMBERLEY ELISABETH GRAY

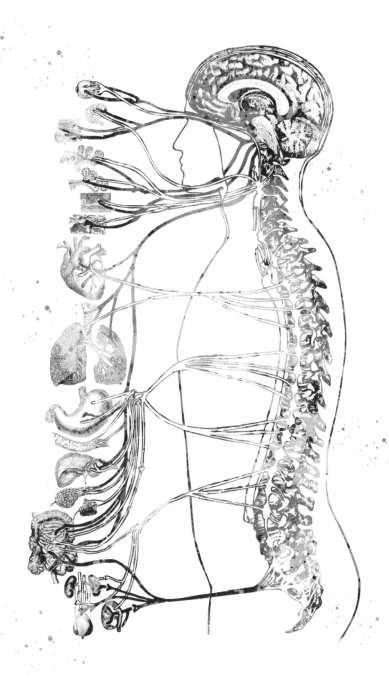

CONTENTS

INTRODUCTION: AWAKENING TO THE INNATE ESSENCE OF YOUR VAGUS NERVE

Imagine a superhighway connecting your mind and body, influencing everything from your moods to digestion and overall vitality— Meet the vagus nerve, the key to unveiling inner harmony.

In a world where stress, anxiety, and feelings of shame have become a near-constant presence and gut health issues seem all too familiar, the discovery of the vagus nerve as a source of healing can feel like finding a hidden, life-changing map. This book, *Vagus Nerve Brain-Belly Reset: Somatic Therapy for Complex PTSD and Gut Health: 40+ Beginner Exercises for Optimal Mind-Body Healing,* is your guide to that map—a journey into the science and practical tools behind one of the body's most potent pathways to mental and physical well-being.

The vagus nerve, stretching from your brainstem through your chest and down to your abdomen, influences everything from how calm or tense you feel to the health of your digestion, immune system, and more. Through this journey, you'll discover how activating the vagus nerve can transform your life by promoting mental calm, enhancing physical health, and cultivating emotional resilience.

The Promise of This Book

Perhaps traditional methods haven't offered the complete relief you're looking for, or you're tired of solutions that only skim the surface of the underlying problem. What you'll learn here isn't a quick fix but a fundamental shift. This book presents research-backed, practical, holistic strategies that can help you connect with your vagus nerve and, in doing so, take control of your health from the inside out.

The vagus nerve holds a unique position in the body as a connector between the brain and the gut, creating a communication line constantly shaping how we feel and function. When it's working well, we're more capable of handling stress, and our bodies tend to experience less inflammation and fewer digestive issues. However, when it's weakened or underactive, the body's natural balance is disrupted, leading to problems that are as mental as they are physical—chronic anxiety, digestive distress, sleep difficulties, and more. This interconnectedness of psychological and physical well-being, mediated by the vagus nerve, is a crucial aspect of our health that we should all be more aware of.

The following pages introduce practical methods for activating the vagus nerve and improving its tone. You'll investigate powerful breathing and somatic exercises, dietary choices, mindfulness practices, and lifestyle adjustments that will stimulate neural pathways shown to alleviate complex PTSD symptoms without the need for extensive treatment. This is not just a book about anatomy or stress relief; it is a toolkit for gaining control over some of the body's most critical processes, allowing you to feel clearer, stronger, and more at ease.

My Condensed, Personal Metamorphosis

To share the path that led to this book, I would like to begin with my personal journey—marked by incessant anxiety and irritable bowel syndrome (IBS) throughout my childhood into my teen and early adult years. My ongoing battles with depression and anxiety have driven me to seek alternative healthcare avenues, which underscores my deep dedication to holistic self-help techniques and ongoing practices.

For years, I found myself caught in cycles of anxiety that seemed to settle in my stomach and spread throughout my entire body. While sometimes helpful, traditional stress management methods left gaps that seemed impossible to fill. I was prescribed countless medications, experimented with different diet plans, made lackadaisical attempts to meditate, sporadically exercised, and dabbled in reading dozens of self-help books. And while some of these efforts offered moments of relief, my dismal health situation remained the same, mainly because my overall sense of self was damaged.

My energy was constantly vibrating at low frequency, and I couldn't seem to find that "zest for life" one needs to create a foundation for lasting positive change. I felt the medical system treated my symptoms without ever caring to get to the root of the problem. Shame was like a lingering shadow continuously tearing at my heart and gut.

Years later, in my mid to late 20s, I recognized and admitted to myself that I had a terrible propensity to use drugs and alcohol as a coping mechanism for stress. My second attempt at inpatient rehab was in 2023. During one of the group therapy sessions, our counselor/psychotherapist shared an article on the healing power of the vagus nerve. We learned that this remarkable neuron, often called the "wandering nerve" for its intricate network reaching far across the body, was shockingly responsible for mental, emotional, physical, and spiritual well-being.

It wasn't just another body part; it was the very system that could help a person cultivate calm, strengthen digestive health, and restore balance to mind, body, and soul. The idea that there was a pathway in my body capable of creating stability and healing was astonishing.

I began researching everything I could about the vagus nerve, reading medical journals, speaking with experts, and experimenting with exercises and diet adjustments that could "tone" this nerve and improve its functioning. And slowly, with each practice, I began to notice changes. The anxiety that had once been a constant companion started to feel more manageable.

My digestion began to feel more settled, I would often wake up feeling more at ease, and I noticed a new sense of resilience in myself—a steadiness that allowed me to handle life's inevitable challenges with a calmness I had never known I could learn to harness.

Now, I feel I have an essential obligation to admit that my personal transformation would not have been possible without a third attempt with inpatient rehabilitation. However, this time, I did not choose to seek conventional rehab therapy. I was desperate for immediate, intense intervention. So I flew to Mexico, where I am forever grateful for two different plant medicines called Ibogaine and 5-MeO-DMT. These psychedelics have the potential to rewire your neural circuitry, or brain chemistry, which makes one much more receptive to the teachings you will learn in this book. I am not condoning psychedelic medication for everyone. But in my state of hopelessness, it enabled me to climb my way out of hell into a life of sobriety and ongoing mind-body healing practices.

Today, I am a registered holistic nutritionist (RHN), personal training specialist (PTS), and I hold a bachelor's degree in psychology from a Canadian University. This journey has been transformative—a personal metamorphosis—and it has become my mission to share what I have discovered about unique healing methods. This book serves as my way of sharing that life-changing journey with you.

A Research-Backed, Holistic Approach

I understand it can be challenging to put faith in a new approach, especially when the world is full of self-help theories and "quick-fix" health trends. This book, however, is built on a foundation of science. In creating this guide, I've drawn from reputable research on the vagus nerve, gut–brain connection, and mind-body healing strategies. I've worked alongside health experts, delved into scientific studies, and combined years of personal experience with practical wisdom to offer you a toolkit that's as credible as it is accessible.

Each chapter introduces simple, actionable steps backed by research and designed for those new to the concept of vagus nerve activation. This process means that the strategies presented here will be easy to adopt, especially for beginners. They're structured to become natural, life-enhancing practices over time.

Now, I invite you to embark on this journey with curiosity and a willingness to explore new theories and approaches to enhance overall well-being. There's no rush or pressure to master everything at once. Instead, each strategy is meant to be tried, tested, and adapted to your unique needs.

Moving Forward With an Open Mind

As you start reading, I encourage you to be open to the possibilities of change. True transformation does not happen overnight, and it is rarely a straight path; however, the methods outlined in this book are gentle, adaptable, and designed to meet you where you are today. Healing often requires a combination of physical, mental, and emotional approaches and this book offers exactly that:

- **Actionable strategies for anxiety relief:** Simple, effective techniques to calm the mind and reduce anxiety, shame, and PTSD symptoms by activating the vagus nerve, including breathwork, meditation, and body movements.
- **Gut health optimization:** Dietary advice, lifestyle adjustments, and supplement guidance to support a healthier microbiome and improved digestion.
- **Mind-body techniques for balance:** Practices that integrate body and mind, helping you cultivate a sense of groundedness and resilience in daily life.

This book is more than a guide; it's a toolkit that gives you the power to reconnect with your body's natural healing rhythms. Each chapter is designed to build upon the last, creating a cumulative effect that strengthens the vagus nerve, balances the gut, and brings clarity to the mind. Together, we'll explore these practices and how they can be woven into your daily life to create meaningful change.

The advantages of a balanced vagus nerve extend beyond individual symptoms; you will likely notice improvements in other aspects of your life. Relationships improve as stress eases. The body becomes more resilient, and emotions begin to feel less overwhelming. This holistic approach doesn't just address one issue; it lays a foundation for a healthier, more harmonious life.

Imagine your life free from the weight of complex PTSD symptoms—a life where your body feels rejuvenated, your mind is clear, your gut is at ease, and you wake up each morning inspired by the person staring back at you in the mirror!

So, as you hold this book in your hands, know that you're holding more than just information—you're holding a path forward. A path to reduced anxiety, improved gut health, and an empowered understanding of your own nervous system. With an open mind and a commitment to trying the strategies you'll learn here, you're ready to embark on a quest for true inner healing.

Disclaimer: This book does not provide medical advice. The content provided is for informational or educational purposes only. Nothing in this book is intended to be a substitute for professional medical advice, diagnosis, or treatment. Always seek the advice of your physician or other qualified healthcare provider with any questions regarding a medical condition or treatment before undertaking a new health or exercise regimen.

What You Can Look Forward To

This book is structured to guide you step-by-step through understanding, activating, and nurturing your vagus nerve to improve mental clarity, alleviate anxiety, prevent feelings of shame, reduce the symptoms of PTSD, and enhance digestive health. Here's a preview of what each chapter holds:

Chapter 1: The Vagus Nerve—Your Mind-Body Gateway to Restored Well-Being: A straightforward exploration of the vagus nerve's key functions and pathways; this chapter explains how it impacts mental health, controls the body's fight, flight, and freeze responses, and forms a crucial link between gut health, immunity, and inflammation.

Chapter 2: Regulating a Dysregulated Vagus Nerve: Identify the physical, emotional, and behavioral signs of poor vagal tone, understand how an underactive vagus nerve disrupts digestion and amplifies anxiety, and learn strategies to energize your vagus nerve. This chapter also delves into common causes of vagus nerve dysfunction, including chronic stress and unhealthy lifestyle habits.

Chapter 3: Holistic Strategies to Energize Vagal Tone and Address the Root Causes of Shame: Master mindful breathwork techniques like diaphragmatic and alternate nostril breathing and engage in meditation practices that quiet mental chatter. Explore lifestyle habits for long-term tranquility, such as daily movement, better sleep, and connecting with nature.

Chapter 4: Dietary Choices for a Harmonized Gut and Optimal Vagal Function: Discover foods that support vagal tone and mental focus, including anti-inflammatory ingredients, healthy fats, and gut-nurturing nutrients.

Learn about the benefits of fermented foods, probiotics, and prebiotics, and understand which foods to avoid for optimal nervous system health.

Chapter 5: Mastering Movement for Enhanced Vagal Tone: This chapter provides guidance on incorporating moderate physical activities like walking and other aerobics, and resistance exercises. Learn about breath-centric stretching disciplines such as yoga, tai chi, and Pilates, and develop a consistent exercise routine that tracks progress and celebrates achievements.

Chapter 6: Parasympathetic Healing Practices for Vagus Nerve Activation: Engage in relaxation techniques such as guided meditation, visualization, and progressive muscle relaxation. Practice sound healing through humming, chanting, and singing, and experience the benefits of gentle cold exposure methods like cold showers and facial immersion.

Chapter 7: Mindset Shifts for Inner Peace: Cultivate a compassionate, growth-focused mindset that embraces self-care, gratitude, and resilience. Build emotional regulation tools through journaling, boundary setting, and stress reduction practices that empower you to face challenges with confidence.

Chapter 8: Crafting Your Lifelong Wellness Journey: Design a personalized wellness plan with clear priorities and balanced routines. Learn to maintain motivation, celebrate progress, and find social support to enhance your journey and inspire those around you.

Conclusion: Embracing a Lifelong Journey of Vagal Health: Reflect on the journey you've undertaken, gain encouragement to stay consistent, and receive a final call to action that empowers you to implement these strategies and share your discoveries.

Let's begin with "Chapter 1: The Vagus Nerve: Your Mind-Body Gateway to Restored Well-Being" and explore the vagus nerve's functions and pathways and its links to your mental and physical health.

1

THE VAGUS NERVE—YOUR MIND-BODY GATEWAY TO RESTORED WELL-BEING

Did you know? The vagus nerve is the body's longest and most powerful nerve network, which has the potential to act as a "refresh" button to gradually soothe inflammation, relax chronic overthinking, and ease digestive distress.

Understanding the vagus nerve's role in overall health is crucial for anyone looking to enhance their mental well-being and physical health. This chapter unravels the basic science behind the vagus nerve, highlighting its structure, function, and importance in the parasympathetic nervous system while detailing its pathways and significant influence on bodily functions. By the end of this section, you will understand why this nerve is key to maintaining mental stability, managing stress, and supporting various body systems.

Science of the Vagus Nerve

What Is the Vagus Nerve?

The vagus nerve, named from the Latin word for "wandering," truly lives up to its name, as it extends from the brainstem down through the chest and into the abdomen, branching out to touch nearly every major organ along the way. It is the longest of the 12 cranial nerves in the body, and its reach provides a unique influence over multiple vital systems, including the cardiovascular, respiratory, and digestive systems.

An integral component of the parasympathetic nervous system, the vagus nerve functions as the main communicator between the brain and various parts of the body. It transmits sensory information from the organs to the brain and relays motor signals back to these organs. This communication is crucial for regulating involuntary processes such as heart rate, digestion, and respiratory rate.

The primary function of the vagus nerve is to act as a central command for the parasympathetic "rest and digest" response, which is in contrast to the "fight or flight" response managed by the sympathetic nervous system. This role positions the vagus nerve as an essential regulator of calmness and recovery, as well as of action and reaction in the body.

Importance in the Parasympathetic Nervous System

The parasympathetic nervous system, often described as the "brake" system of the body, slows down functions that are stimulated by the "accelerator" system or the sympathetic nervous system. The vagus nerve orchestrates this response, promoting relaxation and energy conservation. The "digest" benefit refers to reactivation of the digestive system, which is shut down during the sympathetic response to conserve energy.

When the vagus nerve is stimulated, it signals the release of neurotransmitters such as acetylcholine and gamma-aminobutyric acid (GABA), which help reduce inflammation and promote feelings of calm. This function aids in bringing the body back to a state of balance after periods of stress or high alert.

Influence on Various Bodily Systems

The influence of the vagus nerve extends across many bodily functions:

- **Cardiovascular system:** Regulates heart rate and blood pressure.
- **Digestive system:** Controls the secretion of stomach acids, digestion speed, and motility.
- **Immune system:** Modulates inflammation by signaling the production of anti-inflammatory substances.
- **Respiratory system:** Influences breathing rate and the sensation of "air hunger," the need to breathe.

Key Functions and Pathways

Connection to the Brain and Vital Organs

The vagus nerve plays a significant role in transmitting signals between the brain and major organs such as the heart, lungs, and gut. It serves as a bidirectional superhighway, sending information to the brain about the body's condition and conveying commands back to the organs to maintain homeostasis. Homeostasis is the body's process of maintaining a stable internal environment necessary for sustaining life (Buckley, 2020). This extensive network allows the vagus nerve to coordinate a broad range of physiological processes simultaneously.

Pathways Affecting Mood, Digestion, and Heart Rate

The vagus nerve contributes to mood regulation through its involvement with the gut-brain axis. This complex communication system connects the gut and brain via neural, hormonal, and immune pathways. The gut is sometimes called the "second brain" because of its vast network of neurons, and the vagus nerve acts as the bridge linking these two centers. When vagal tone (the strength of the nerve's activity) is high, it can help enhance mood and stabilize emotions by influencing neurotransmitter levels such as serotonin, which is predominantly produced in the gut.

The vagus nerve also helps regulate the heart rate by slowing it down when necessary. This process is another form of vagal tone, and it reflects the nerve's capacity to foster a state of calm. A higher vagal tone is associated with a greater ability to recover from stress and manage heart health.

Role in the "Rest and Digest" Function: Parasympathetic State

When the vagus nerve activates the parasympathetic state, the body experiences a cascade of calming effects: heart rate slows, digestion becomes more efficient, and blood pressure lowers. This state is critical for proper digestion and nutrient absorption. The activation of this state also helps reduce cortisol levels, supporting the body's ability to unwind after stress.

Why the Vagus Nerve Matters for Mental Health

Connection to Mood Stabilization

The vagus nerve's impact on mental health stems from its role in modulating the body's response to stress. By stimulating the production of calming neurotransmitters and engaging the parasympathetic nervous system, the vagus nerve helps promote mood stabilization. This response can mitigate the feelings of anxiety and agitation often triggered by a hyperactive sympathetic nervous system.

The vagus nerve's tone, or activity level, is a predictor of how well a person can adapt to stress and recover from it. Research indicates that a higher vagal tone corresponds with a more positive mood, lower levels of anxiety and shame, reduced symptoms of PTSD, and greater emotional resilience (Breit et al., 2018).

Regulation of Cortisol Levels

Cortisol, which you now know as the "stress hormone," is released in response to stress and has various effects on the body, including heightened alertness and increased blood sugar. While necessary in acute situations, chronic high levels of cortisol can lead to anxiety, weight gain, and impaired immune function. The vagus nerve helps keep cortisol levels in check by promoting relaxation and dampening the stress response. This is achieved through its influence on the hypothalamic-pituitary-adrenal (HPA) axis, which regulates stress responses (Thayer & Lane, 2009).

Implications for Anxiety and Stress Management

Strengthening vagal tone has been shown to be an effective way to manage anxiety and stress. This is because a well-toned vagus nerve encourages the body to enter the "rest and digest" mode more quickly after a stressful event. Techniques such as deep breathing, meditation, and even humming can stimulate the vagus nerve and improve its function (Laborde et al., 2017). These and other calming techniques will be explained in subsequent chapters.

The role of the vagus nerve in managing anxiety also extends to the regulation of the gut. Since the gut and brain communicate closely through the vagus nerve, a healthy gut can support better mental health, while an unhealthy gut may exacerbate feelings of anxiety and stress. This two-way relationship underscores the importance of practices that maintain both vagus nerve health and gut integrity.

How the Vagus Nerve Affects Mental Health

The vagus nerve plays a central role in connecting the mind and body, significantly influencing how we respond to stress, manage emotions, and maintain mental health. Understanding its function in mental health provides valuable insight into why some people are more resilient under pressure and how certain interventions can improve emotional stability. This section explores the vagus nerve's role in response patterns to stress, emotional regulation, and the importance of enhancing vagal tone for a balanced, calm state of mind.

Our Fight, Flight, and Freeze Response Patterns

The fight, flight, and freeze responses are the body's instinctive reactions to perceived threats. These responses are governed by the autonomic nervous system (ANS), which comprises the sympathetic nervous system (SNS) and the parasympathetic nervous system (PNS), which were discussed in the previous section. While the SNS triggers fight or flight, preparing the body for action by increasing heart rate and releasing stress hormones, the PNS—led by the vagus nerve—regulates the "freeze" response and helps return the body to a state of rest.

Relationship Between Vagus Activity and Anxiety

The balance between sympathetic and parasympathetic activity is crucial for mental well-being. An underactive or dysfunctional vagus nerve can lead to an overactive SNS, making it difficult to switch off stress responses. This prolonged activation can contribute to anxiety disorders and chronic stress, as the body remains in a heightened state of alertness without sufficient regulation. Individuals with lower vagal tone often struggle more with shame or increased or persistent symptoms of Complex PTSD as their bodies are less efficient at de-escalating from the fight or flight state (Porges, 2007).

How Vagal Tone Impacts Resilience to Stress

Vagal tone refers to the activity level of the vagus nerve and serves as an indicator of how well the PNS can modulate the stress response. A high vagal tone is associated with a quicker return to baseline after stress, enabling a person to recover more effectively. Those with higher vagal tone demonstrate better resilience to stress and are more capable of maintaining composure in challenging situations (Thayer & Lane, 2000). Conversely, individuals with a low vagal tone may find it harder to calm down, leading to prolonged stress and increased risk of mental health issues. These are clear indications of the physical influence on the mind and mood!

Indicators of Vagus Nerve Dysfunction

Signs of vagus nerve dysfunction can manifest in both physical and emotional ways. Common indicators include:

- persistent anxiety, worry, and feelings of shame
- increased or persistent symptoms of complex PTSD
- difficulty managing stress
- digestive issues such as IBS
- chronic fatigue
- heightened sensitivity to pain

Recognizing these signs is essential for addressing the underlying issue and taking steps to improve vagal tone.

The Vagus Nerve and Emotional Regulation

The vagus nerve's influence extends into emotional regulation, impacting how we process and recover from stress and trauma. The nerve's ability to promote a calming effect through the PNS means that it plays a significant role in regulating emotions and fostering psychological resilience.

Role in Managing Reactions to Trauma and Stress

The body's response to trauma is complex and often involves hyperarousal, where the nervous system remains on high alert. The vagus nerve helps moderate this response by facilitating a shift from heightened arousal to a state of safety and calm. Techniques that stimulate the vagus nerve, such as deep breathing and mindfulness, can activate the PNS and assist in down-regulating the body's response to trauma (Porges, 2011).

How the Vagus Nerve Supports Resilience and Recovery From Emotional Setbacks

Resilience is the capacity to adapt to stress and bounce back from emotional challenges. The vagus nerve plays a central role in this process. When it functions optimally, it helps the brain regulate emotions more efficiently, making it easier to navigate setbacks and reduce the likelihood of prolonged emotional distress. High vagal tone promotes effective emotional regulation by fostering a more adaptive response to stressors (Laborde et al., 2017). It essentially primes the body and mind to better handle future challenges by creating a feedback loop of calm and recovery. A toned vagus nerve helps alleviate shame and diminish the complex symptoms of PTSD.

Benefits of a Well-Toned Vagus Nerve for Emotional Stability

A well-toned vagus nerve contributes to emotional stability in several ways:

- **Reduced reactivity to stress:** A well-functioning vagus nerve allows the body to disengage more quickly from a stress response.
- **Enhanced mood regulation:** High vagal tone is linked to the regulation of neurotransmitters like serotonin and dopamine, which influence mood and emotional health.
- **Better interpersonal interactions:** The nerve's regulation of the body's state affects how we connect and respond to others, fostering more balanced social interactions.

Enhancing Calm With Vagal Tone

Improving vagal tone involves engaging in practices that activate the PNS, fostering mental clarity, and promoting overall well-being.

How Vagal Tone Fosters Mental Clarity

When the vagus nerve is stimulated, it promotes the release of acetylcholine, a neurotransmitter that reduces the body's stress response and enhances cognitive function. This allows for greater mental clarity, improved decision-making, and a general sense of calm. A high vagal tone supports clear thinking by decreasing the noise of anxious thoughts and creating space for a more focused mindset.

Connection to Positive Mental Health Outcomes

High vagal tone has been correlated with positive mental health outcomes such as reduced anxiety, lower stress levels, and better emotional regulation (Kok & Fredrickson, 2010). Studies show that practices that enhance vagal tone, such as yoga, deep diaphragmatic breathing, and meditation, contribute to long-term improvements in mood and mental stability. Enhanced vagal activity also supports heart rate variability (HRV), an indicator of autonomic balance and a predictor of overall health and stress resilience.

Real-Life Benefits of Increased Vagal Tone

People with improved vagal tone often report tangible mental and physical benefits, including:

- **Increased relaxation and peace of mind:** Regular stimulation of the vagus nerve helps individuals manage stress more effectively, resulting in a state of ongoing calm.
- **Better sleep quality:** Enhanced vagal tone supports the body's ability to relax, facilitating more restful sleep and improved energy levels.
- **Improved social connectedness:** A high vagal tone fosters social bonding, which is essential for mental health and emotional resilience. It enhances the capacity for empathy and improves social interactions by regulating physiological responses

during conversations and social engagements (Porges, 2009).

Real-life applications can be as simple as integrating practices like slow, deep breathing into daily routines. Consistent engagement in such practices encourages the vagus nerve to maintain a balanced and calm state, supporting steady, unvarying overall mental and emotional health.

Our Gut-Brain Connection

The relationship between our gut and brain is more intertwined than once thought, connected by a complex network that allows them to communicate bidirectionally. This communication impacts both physical and mental health, influencing everything from mood regulation to digestive efficiency. The vagus nerve serves as a critical bridge in this system, facilitating a constant exchange of information between the gut and the brain. Understanding how this connection works can illuminate why gut health is vital for overall mental well-being and how vagal tone plays a significant role in maintaining this balance.

Your Vagus Nerve as a Bridge

Pathway From the Gut to the Brain and Vice Versa

The vagus nerve is a primary channel through which the gut and brain communicate. This nerve, which is the longest cranial nerve in the body, extends from the brainstem through the neck, chest, and abdomen, directly connecting to major organs, including the intestines. Through its sensory and motor pathways, the vagus nerve relays information about the state of the gut to the brain and sends commands back that regulate digestion and emotional responses.

The vagus nerve's sensory fibers detect changes in the gut environment, such as the presence of specific bacteria or alterations in the gut lining. These signals are transmitted to the brain, which interprets and responds to them, influencing mood, stress levels, and overall mental health. Conversely, the brain sends signals through the vagus nerve to modulate gut function, including peristalsis (the movement of food through the intestines) and the secretion of digestive enzymes (Bonaz et al., 2018).

How Gut Health Influences Mental Health

The gut, often referred to as the "second brain," plays a pivotal role in mental health due to the production of neurotransmitters like serotonin and dopamine. About 90% of the body's serotonin—a neurotransmitter linked to feelings of well-being—is produced in the gut. Disruptions in gut health can affect the production and balance of these neurotransmitters, contributing to mood disorders, including anxiety and depression, shame, and the symptoms of complex PTSD (Carabotti et al., 2015). The vagus nerve acts as the highway that conveys gut conditions to the brain, directly impacting emotional and psychological states.

Vagus Nerve's Role in Gut–Brain Communication

The vagus nerve facilitates a feedback loop between the gut and the brain that is essential for maintaining homeostasis. For instance, when the gut encounters an imbalance, such as an overgrowth of harmful bacteria, the vagus nerve communicates this information to the brain, which can trigger a response that affects mood and behavior. Conversely, stress and emotional turmoil can disrupt gut function, leading to symptoms like nausea or IBS. This intricate communication pathway underscores the importance of maintaining a healthy vagal tone for both mental and gut health (Breit et al., 2018).

Vagus Nerve and Digestive Health

How the Nerve Regulates Digestive Function

The vagus nerve plays a fundamental role in digestion by managing the release of stomach acid, bile production, and intestinal movement. This nerve ensures that food is processed efficiently, and it signals the muscles of the stomach and intestines to contract and relax, the process of peristalsis, propelling food along the digestive tract. Additionally, the vagus nerve helps stimulate the secretion of digestive enzymes that break down food into nutrients, enabling the body to absorb essential vitamins and minerals (Mönnikes, 2016).

A well-functioning vagus nerve supports smooth and efficient digestion. However, when vagal tone is low, the nerve's ability to regulate these processes diminishes, resulting in issues like bloating, constipation, or more severe conditions such as gastroparesis. A disrupted digestive process can lead to nutrient deficiencies and an impaired gut lining, which further exacerbates health problems.

Importance of a Balanced Gut Microbiome

The gut microbiome—the collection of trillions of microorganisms living in the intestines—has a significant impact on both digestion and brain function. A healthy gut microbiome supports optimal digestion and boosts the immune system, which is intertwined with the vagus nerve's regulatory role. Beneficial bacteria in the gut produce short-chain fatty acids

(SCFAs) that promote vagus nerve stimulation, leading to enhanced communication between the gut and brain (Fülling et al., 2019). This interaction contributes to improved mood and cognitive function.

An imbalance in the gut microbiome, known as dysbiosis, can lead to inflammation and negatively affect vagus nerve function. This disruption can manifest as digestive disorders and heightened anxiety, highlighting the importance of maintaining a balanced microbiome for mental and digestive health.

Link Between Poor Vagal Tone and Digestive Disorders

Low vagal tone can impair the body's ability to manage the "rest and digest" response effectively. This dysfunction has been linked to various digestive issues, including IBS, which affects the large intestine and can lead to pain, bloating, and irregular bowel movements. Individuals with poor vagal tone may experience a chronic, low-level stress response that exacerbates these symptoms, perpetuating a cycle of discomfort and anxiety (Bonaz et al., 2016).

Impacts on Immunity and Inflammation

Connection to Immune System Regulation

The vagus nerve plays a pivotal role in regulating the immune system. Through its influence on the cholinergic (acetylcholine or butyrylcholine neurotransmitters) anti-inflammatory pathway, the vagus nerve helps modulate the body's inflammatory response. When the vagus nerve is activated, it signals immune cells to produce anti-inflammatory cytokines, proteins that reduce inflammation. This modulation helps keep the body's immune response in check, preventing excessive inflammation that could lead to chronic conditions (Pavlov & Tracey, 2017).

How Vagus Nerve Activity Impacts Inflammation

Inflammation is a natural response to injury or infection, but chronic inflammation is linked to a host of health problems, including autoimmune diseases, mental health disorders, and cardiovascular issues. The vagus nerve helps prevent the immune system from overreacting, reducing the risk of inflammation becoming chronic. Studies have shown that stimulating the vagus nerve can reduce markers of inflammation in the body, supporting overall health and preventing conditions like rheumatoid arthritis and inflammatory bowel disease (IBD) (Tracey, 2009).

Role in Chronic Inflammatory Conditions Like IBS, Which Can Lead to Increased Anxiety

Chronic inflammation in the gut, such as that seen in IBS, has far-reaching implications beyond digestive discomfort. It can increase the permeability of the gut lining, allowing harmful substances to enter the bloodstream, a condition known as "leaky gut." This can lead to systemic inflammation, which is associated with increased stress, shame, and increased or persistent complex symptoms of PTSD. The vagus nerve's anti-inflammatory action is crucial for preventing and managing these conditions. Poor vagal tone can make it difficult for the body to regulate inflammation, exacerbating both digestive and psychological symptoms (Bonaz et al., 2017).

For individuals suffering from IBS and related disorders, interventions that stimulate the vagus nerve, such as deep breathing exercises, meditation, and specific dietary changes, have been shown to reduce both gut inflammation and anxiety levels. By engaging in practices that enhance vagal tone, it is possible to break the cycle of chronic inflammation anxiety, shame, and symptoms of PTSD, leading to better gut health and emotional stability.

Chapter 1 Summary

The long, diverse vagus nerve facilitates communications through the brain-gut axis, helping manage stress and inflammation. A well-toned vagus nerve ensures emotional and physical stability and contributes to improved mood and overall health.

- **Introduction to the vagus nerve:**
  - longest cranial nerve, connecting the brainstem to major organs in the body
  - central to the parasympathetic nervous system, responsible for the "rest and digest" response
- **Key functions and pathways:**
  - facilitates communication between the brain and vital organs, including the heart, lungs, and digestive system
  - helps regulate heart rate, digestion, and respiratory rate
  - plays a significant role in maintaining homeostasis and overall health
- **Influence on mental health:**
  - high vagal tone is linked to better stress management and emotional resilience
  - regulates cortisol levels, reducing chronic stress and promoting mood stability
  - aids in recovery from the fight, flight, and freeze responses

- **Indicators of vagus nerve dysfunction:**
  - low vagal tone can manifest as anxiety, chronic stress, shame, digestive problems, and fatigue
  - increased or persistent symptoms of Complex PTSD
  - recognizing signs of poor vagal tone can help in targeting effective interventions
- **Benefits of a well-toned vagus nerve:**
  - supports emotional stability, resilience to stress, and mental clarity
  - enhances mood regulation and reduces symptoms of anxiety
  - contributes to a balanced gut-brain connection for better overall health

Let's progress to "Chapter 2: Recognizing the Signs of a Dysregulated Vagus Nerve" to give you insights into your own mind and body reactions to the consequences of stress and other disruptors.

RECOGNIZING THE SIGNS OF A DYSREGULATED VAGUS NERVE

What can, at times, feel like never-ending anxiety, painful digestive issues, brain fog, and absent-mindedness... Could the vagus nerve be the missing piece of our wellness puzzle?

Signs of Poor Vagal Tone

A well-functioning vagus nerve plays a critical role in regulating stress responses, supporting digestion, and maintaining emotional balance. When the vagal tone is low or the vagus nerve is dysregulated, it can lead to a host of physical, mental, and emotional issues. This section outlines the key signs of poor vagal tone, helping individuals identify when their nervous system may be out of balance.

Physical Indicators

Chronic Digestive Issues

One of the most common physical manifestations of poor vagal tone is chronic digestive problems. The vagus nerve helps regulate the process of digestion, controlling stomach acid production, peristalsis (the movement of food through the digestive tract), and the secretion of digestive enzymes. When the vagus nerve's activity is impaired, digestion slows down, leading to symptoms such as bloating, constipation, and indigestion (Breit et al., 2018).

Conditions like IBS are often associated with dysregulation of the gut–brain axis, where poor vagal tone contributes to heightened gut sensitivity and altered motility. A compromised vagus nerve disrupts the balance between the parasympathetic and sympathetic nervous systems, making it harder for the body to enter a relaxed, efficient state for digestion and overall function.

Tension Headaches and Fatigue

Low vagal tone can also result in tension headaches and persistent fatigue. The vagus nerve's influence on the cardiovascular and respiratory systems means that poor vagal activity can affect blood circulation and oxygen delivery throughout the body. This can lead to chronic tension-type headaches, which may be accompanied by feelings of tiredness that don't improve with rest. Such symptoms are tied to the body's inability to fully switch to a restorative state and recover from stress (Thayer & Lane, 2009).

Physical Symptoms Tied to Stress

Physical stress responses are magnified when the vagus nerve is dysregulated. Symptoms like rapid heartbeat, shallow breathing, muscle tension, and digestive distress may persist longer than they should after a stressful event. This prolonged physical arousal is due to the vagus nerve's reduced ability to engage the parasympathetic "brake" that calms the body.

When the vagus nerve struggles to counterbalance the "fight or flight" response, the body remains in a heightened state, contributing to long-term health issues such as high blood pressure and chronic inflammation (Porges, 2011).

Mental Health Symptoms

Persistent Anxiety and Mood Swings

One of the clearest indicators of poor vagal tone is persistent anxiety. The vagus nerve is involved in regulating the stress response by managing cortisol levels, the body's primary stress hormone. When vagal tone is low, the body struggles to return to a baseline state after stress, resulting in prolonged anxiety and chronic worry, feelings of shame, and increased or persistent symptoms of complex PTSD (Laborde et al., 2017).

Mood swings are another mental health symptom of vagal dysfunction. The inability of the vagus nerve to modulate positive feeling neurotransmitter levels like serotonin and dopamine contributes to inconsistent mood regulation. This can make a person more susceptible to emotional highs and lows, leaving them feeling on edge or irritable without a clear reason.

Difficulty Recovering From Stress

Recovery from stress is an essential part of maintaining mental health. Individuals with strong vagal tone can typically bounce back from stress more quickly, experiencing a smooth transition from a state of arousal to a state of calm. Those with poor vagal tone, however, often find it difficult to wind down after a stressful event, remaining in a state of heightened alertness for longer periods (Thayer & Sternberg, 2006). This impaired recovery can contribute to chronic stress, eventually leading to burnout, chronic inflammation, or other mental and physical health issues.

Irritability and Emotional Sensitivity

Irritability and an increased sensitivity to emotional stimuli are common signs of poor vagal tone. When the vagus nerve is not functioning optimally, the body's threshold for stress is lowered, making it harder to handle everyday challenges. People with a low vagal tone may find themselves overreacting to minor irritants or feeling emotionally overwhelmed by situations that others might handle with ease (or that they would better manage if their vagal tone was better). This heightened reactivity can strain relationships and contribute to feelings of social isolation.

Emotional and Behavioral Patterns

Self-Sabotaging Habits and Destructive Coping Mechanisms

Poor vagal tone is often linked to patterns of behavior that can be described as self-sabotaging or destructive. These include habits such as procrastination, substance abuse, and emotional or compulsive overeating, which may be attempts to self-regu-late an overstimulated nervous system. Individuals with low vagal tone may feel the need to engage in these behaviors as a way to numb stress or provide temporary relief, which ultimately exacerbates their mental and physical health issues (Porges, 2017).

Difficulty Finding Calm or Focus

An underactive vagus nerve can make finding moments of calm or focus extremely difficult. The vagus nerve helps the brain switch into a state conducive to concentration and relaxation by controlling the parasympathetic response. When this mechanism is compromised, the mind remains cluttered and scattered, making it challenging to engage in focused activities or feel at ease. This state can lead to difficulties in work, school, and other daily tasks that require focus and sustained attention.

Emotional Reactivity and Social Withdrawal

Emotional reactivity is another common issue for individuals with poor vagal tone. The inability to regulate emotions effectively can make social interactions difficult, leading to feelings of shame or frustration when one reacts more intensely than intended. Over time, this can lead to social withdrawal as a protective mechanism, further reducing emotional and social well-being.

A poorly functioning vagus nerve also impacts a person's ability to express emotions in a balanced way, leading to swings between numbness and overwhelming emotion. This dysregulation affects social connectedness, making it harder to form and maintain healthy relationships. Since social support is crucial for mental health, this withdrawal can contribute to a cycle of isolation and emotional distress.

Struggles With Regulating Emotions

The vagus nerve plays a central role in emotional regulation by influencing the limbic system, which processes emotions. When the vagal tone is low, individuals may struggle to regulate their emotions effectively, leading to a pattern of heightened reactivity followed by emotional exhaustion. This inability to manage emotions contributes to an increased risk of anxiety, depression, and other mental health disorders (Porges, 2009).

Enhanced vagal tone supports a balanced emotional response by promoting the release of calming neurotransmitters and enabling the body to switch more smoothly between emotional states. In contrast, poor vagal tone leaves individuals susceptible to sudden emotional shifts and a reduced ability to handle life's challenges.

How a Dormant Vagus Nerve Disrupts Digestion

The vagus nerve is essential for regulating various bodily functions, including digestion. When it is underactive or "dormant," a host of digestive issues can arise. This section will explore the gut symptoms related to poor vagal tone, how anxiety is linked to digestive health, shame, symptoms of Complex PTSD, and the immune and inflammatory reactions that can be triggered by a poorly functioning vagus nerve. Understanding these impacts can guide effective interventions to restore vagal function and improve overall well-being.

Gut Symptoms Related to Poor Vagal Tone

Constipation, Bloating, and Irregularity

One of the primary roles of the vagus nerve in digestion is regulating peristalsis, the rhythmic contraction of muscles that move food through the digestive tract. When the vagal tone is low, these contractions can become inefficient, leading to constipation, bloating, and irregular bowel movements (Breit et al., 2018). A dormant vagus nerve disrupts the natural pace of the digestive system, causing the food to move too slowly through the intestines, which can result in excessive fermentation, gas production, and discomfort.

Chronic constipation and bloating not only affect physical comfort but can also impact mental health by increasing feelings of distress and irritability. The body's inability to efficiently move waste can exacerbate toxic buildup, further stressing the system and leading to a cycle of poor digestion and declining health.

Low Stomach Acid and Poor Nutrient Absorption

Another critical function of the vagus nerve is stimulating the production of stomach acid and digestive enzymes. When the vagus nerve is underactive, stomach acid levels can drop, leading to hypochlorhydria (a low stomach acid condition). Adequate levels of stomach acid are necessary for breaking down food and absorbing nutrients effectively. When acid levels are too low, proteins may not be digested fully, resulting in nutrient deficiencies, particularly in essential vitamins and minerals such as B12, magnesium, and iron.

Poor nutrient absorption has a cascading effect on overall health, as essential nutrients are needed for energy, cognitive function, and immune support. An underactive vagus nerve thus contributes to a weakened system that struggles with fatigue, reduced immunity, and cognitive sluggishness.

Irritable Bowel Syndrome Connections

IBS is one of the most studied conditions connected to poor vagal tone. IBS is characterized by symptoms such as abdominal pain, cramping, and irregular bowel movements. Research has shown that a dysregulated gut–brain axis, with impaired vagal signaling, can lead to these symptoms becoming chronic and severe (Carabotti et al., 2015).

IBS is not only a physical condition but also has strong psychological components. People with IBS often experience higher levels of anxiety and depression, likely due to the close interplay between gut health and mental health. The vagus nerve, when functioning optimally, can help mediate these symptoms through its influence on the gut–brain connection. Poor vagal tone, however, can result in persistent digestive dysfunction and a heightened perception of pain, further contributing to anxiety and stress.

Linking Anxiety With Digestive Health

Understanding "Butterflies in the Stomach"

The sensation of "butterflies in the stomach" is a well-known example of how emotional states can affect the gut. This feeling arises from the gut–brain connection, where the vagus nerve acts as the communication bridge. Anxiety triggers the sympathetic nervous system, causing the body to enter a state of fight or flight. In this state, digestive processes slow down or stop, allowing the body to divert energy toward dealing with the perceived threat (Porges, 2009). There can be increased or persistent symptoms of Complex PTSD.

When the vagus nerve's calming influence is impaired, the body struggles to switch back to a relaxed state where digestion can resume normally. This delay can lead to symptoms such as nausea, cramping, and bloating, especially in stressful situations.

How Stress Intensifies Digestive Issues

Chronic stress can significantly impair vagal function. When stress is prolonged, it triggers the continuous release of cortisol, the body's main stress hormone. High levels of cortisol can negatively affect the gut lining, causing inflammation and increased gut permeability, known as a "leaky gut" (Camilleri, 2019). This condition allows harmful substances to pass into the bloodstream, leading to systemic inflammation and contributing to digestive issues such as bloating, pain, and diarrhea.

Furthermore, chronic stress reduces the body's ability to produce digestive enzymes and stomach acid, exacerbating existing conditions of hypochlorhydria, a deficiency of stomach acid. If you don't have enough stomach acid, you can't digest food properly or absorb its nutrients. This ongoing cycle of stress and impaired digestion can perpetuate both physical and emotional discomfort.

Cycle of Stress and Digestive Dysfunction

When the vagus nerve is unable to fulfill its regulatory role effectively, it contributes to a vicious cycle. Stress leads to digestive dysfunction, and poor digestion further amplifies stress due to discomfort and the subsequent release of inflammatory cytokines (Pavlov & Tracey, 2017). The continuous interplay between an underactive vagus nerve and gut health can create a loop where symptoms of stress and digestive problems feed into each other, making recovery difficult without targeted intervention.

Immune and Inflammatory Reactions

Autoimmune Connections

The vagus nerve is deeply involved in the regulation of the immune system. It exerts its influence through the cholinergic anti-inflammatory pathway, which helps keep the immune response in check and prevents excessive inflammation. When the vagus nerve is underactive, this regulation can weaken, increasing the risk of destructive autoimmune responses where the body mistakenly attacks its tissues (Bonaz et al., 2018).

Conditions like rheumatoid arthritis, Crohn's disease, and ulcerative colitis have been associated with poor vagal tone. These autoimmune conditions can exacerbate both physical pain and emotional distress, forming a feedback loop that impedes recovery and well-being.

Increased Inflammatory Markers

Chronic low-grade inflammation is linked to a variety of health problems, including digestive disorders and mental health issues. Poor vagal function can lead to increased levels of pro-inflammatory markers such as C-reactive protein (CRP) and tumor necrosis factor-alpha (TNF-α) (Tracey, 2009). These inflammatory markers are not just a result of physical health conditions but also contribute to the worsening of symptoms by perpetuating stress and immune system overactivity.

How a Dysregulated Vagus Nerve Exacerbates Symptoms

A dormant or poorly functioning vagus nerve cannot adequately modulate the body's inflammatory response, leading to chronic inflammation. This exacerbates symptoms related to digestive health, including bloating, cramping, and irregular bowel movements. For those with pre-existing conditions like IBS or leaky gut, poor vagal tone can intensify the inflammatory response, making it difficult to manage symptoms and maintain overall health.

Chronic inflammation affects more than just digestion; it has systemic implications that can lead to fatigue, joint pain, and cognitive difficulties. These symptoms can further heighten stress and anxiety, creating a cycle that impacts mental and physical health. By understanding how the vagus nerve functions and recognizing the signs of poor vagal tone, targeted approaches can be taken to stimulate and improve its activity, ultimately breaking this damaging cycle.

Root Causes of Vagus Nerve Dysfunction

Understanding the root causes of vagus nerve dysfunction is essential for developing strategies to restore its function and maintain overall well-being. The vagus nerve plays a critical role in regulating the parasympathetic nervous system, which controls the body's ability to rest, digest, and recover.

When the vagus nerve becomes impaired or dysregulated, it can lead to a diversity of physical, emotional, and mental health issues. This section explores the main factors that contribute to vagus nerve dysfunction, including chronic stress and trauma, harmful lifestyle choices, and modern-day stressors.

Chronic Stress and Trauma

Long-Term Stress Impacts

Chronic stress is a significant contributor to vagus nerve dysfunction. When the body experiences stress, the sympathetic nervous system activates the "fight or flight" response, releasing stress hormones like cortisol and adrenaline. While short-term activation of this system is a normal response to danger, prolonged exposure can lead to negative outcomes. Chronic stress keeps the body in a constant state of high alert, which can suppress the vagus nerve's function and weaken its tone (Breit et al., 2018).

An underactive vagus nerve means that the parasympathetic response—the body's natural counterbalance to stress—is weakened. This can result in physical symptoms like increased heart rate, high blood pressure, and impaired digestion, as well as mental health issues such as anxiety and depression (Thayer & Lane, 2000).

Connection Between Trauma and Vagus Nerve

Trauma has a profound impact on the nervous system and can leave lasting effects on vagus nerve function. Traumatic experiences, whether physical or emotional, can trigger a persistent state of hyperarousal in the nervous system. This state is characterized by increased activity in the sympathetic nervous system and reduced activity in the parasympathetic system, impairing the vagus nerve's regulatory functions (Porges, 2009).

Trauma can lead to a condition known as "dorsal vagal shutdown," where the vagus nerve response shifts to an extreme state of immobilization or "freeze" response. This response is associated with feelings of numbness, dissociation, and a sense of helplessness.

These long-lasting effects can disrupt emotional regulation and contribute to chronic health issues (van der Kolk, 2014). In the animal kingdom, freezing when threatened is often called "playing dead." It is a defense mechanism when the creature senses it cannot safely escape.

PTSD: An Extreme Result of Trauma

PTSD is a mental health condition caused by "An extremely stressful or terrifying event—either being part of it or witnessing it. Symptoms may include flashbacks, nightmares, severe anxiety and uncontrollable thoughts about the event" (Mayo Clinic Staff, 2024). PTSD is often associated with combat veterans and rescue workers, but it can affect anyone at any time and interfere with social and work situations, leading to a prolonged sense of shame and feelings of undefinable anxiety.

PTSD can cause negative thoughts about yourself or other people, emotions of fear, blame, guilt, anger, or shame, problems with memory (which may include repression of recalling traumatic events), detachment from family and friends, and a loss of interest in previously enjoyed activities.

PTSD vs. Complex PTSD

PTSD generally results from a single traumatic event, like experiencing a car crash, sexual or other physical violence, serious injury, or the death of a close relative, friend, or associate. C-PTSD is more likely the consequence of prolonged trauma, especially during formative years that may last for weeks, months, or even years. Causes may range from continuous child abuse, domestic violence, or intimidation to prolonged exposure to military combat.

Symptoms of PTSD and C-PTSD may be similar, including anxiety, depression, or feelings of shame. But there can be differences: PTSD may cause intrusions of memories of the traumatic event or avoidances of places or activities that recall the event, while C-PTSD has a deeper impact on identity and relationships and may provoke bouts of irritation, anger, lack of emotional control, and feelings of sadness or hopelessness.

Despite the differences, both PTSD and C-PTSD respond positively to activities that tone the vagus nerve and induce a calming parasympathetic response.

Lasting Effects on Nervous System Function

Long-term stress and trauma can result in changes to the nervous system's structure and function. This includes alterations in the brain areas that regulate emotional responses, such as the amygdala and prefrontal cortex. The vagus nerve's weakened state exacerbates these effects, making it harder for individuals to switch from a stressed state to a relaxed state (McEwen, 2007). Consequently, the vagus nerve's impaired function contributes to a cycle of chronic stress and reduced resilience to future stressors.

Harmful Lifestyle Choices

Diet and Its Impact on the Vagus Nerve

Diet plays a crucial role in maintaining vagus nerve health. Foods high in refined sugars, processed ingredients, and unhealthy fats can lead to inflammation, which can impair the vagus nerve's functioning. In contrast, a diet rich in anti-inflammatory foods such as fruits, vegetables, whole grains, nuts, seeds, lean proteins, and omega-3 fatty acids supports vagal tone and overall nervous system health (Mischoulon & Freeman, 2013).

Probiotic-rich foods—loaded with beneficial microbes—and a healthy gut microbiome are also essential for optimal vagus nerve function. The gut–brain axis, mediated by the vagus nerve, relies on a balanced microbiome to send positive signals to the brain. Dysbiosis, or an imbalance of gut bacteria, can negatively affect this communication, contributing to poor vagal tone and associated health issues (Carabotti et al., 2015).

Lack of Exercise or Poor Sleep Habits

Physical inactivity and poor sleep habits can significantly impact vagus nerve health. Regular physical activity, particularly activities that promote mindful movement, like yoga and tai chi, can enhance vagal tone and improve the body's ability to manage stress (Laborde et al., 2017). Conversely, a sedentary lifestyle can reduce vagal tone, making it harder for the body to return to a calm state after stress.

Sleep is another critical factor. During sleep, the body activates the parasympathetic nervous system to promote healing and recovery. Chronic sleep deprivation disrupts this process, leading to elevated stress levels, impaired immune function, and reduced vagal activity (Kahn et al., 2013). Ensuring consistent, high-quality sleep is essential for maintaining a healthy vagus nerve and overall well-being. At least seven hours of sleep are recommended nightly; no exceptions for weekends!

Substance Use (Alcohol, Drugs) and Overstimulation

Substance use, including excessive alcohol and drug consumption, can negatively affect the vagus nerve. These substances interfere with the body's natural neurotransmitter functions, impairing the nervous system's ability to maintain balance. Alcohol, for instance, can lead to decreased vagal tone by inhibiting the parasympathetic response, contributing to increased anxiety and poor emotional regulation (Mayfield et al., 2008).

Overstimulation from too much caffeine and other stimulants also puts strain on the nervous system. These substances can increase heart rate and blood pressure, counteracting the calming influence of the vagus nerve. Regular use of stimulants can lead to a state of constant overactivation, reducing the body's ability to engage in rest and digest processes.

Modern-Day Stressors

Technology and Screen Time

In the digital age, technology and excessive screen time have become significant stressors that affect vagus nerve health. The overuse of digital devices can lead to overstimulation of the nervous system, contributing to disrupted sleep patterns, increased anxiety, and difficulty focusing. Blue light exposure from screens interferes with the production of melatonin, the hormone that regulates sleep, leading to sleep disruption and decreased vagal activity (Chang et al., 2015).

The constant influx of information and notifications also triggers a state of hyperarousal in the brain, making it difficult to relax and engage the parasympathetic response. To mitigate these effects, incorporating screen-free periods and practicing digital detox can help reset the nervous system and support vagal tone. This includes no screen time before going to sleep.

Environmental Toxins

Exposure to environmental toxins, such as air pollution, pesticides, and heavy metals, can adversely affect the vagus nerve. These toxins contribute to systemic inflammation and oxidative stress, which can impair nervous system function and weaken the vagus nerve's ability to regulate bodily processes (Block & Calderón-Garcidueñas, 2009). Reducing exposure to toxins and incorporating antioxidants into the diet can help combat inflammation and support vagal health.

Social Stressors and Isolation

Social connection plays a vital role in maintaining vagus nerve health. Positive social interactions stimulate the vagus nerve, promoting a sense of safety and well-being. Conversely, chronic social stressors, such as conflict, workplace pressure, and social isolation, can reduce vagal tone and increase stress levels (Holt-Lunstad et al., 2010). The COVID-19 pandemic, for example, has amplified social isolation and its effects on mental health, demonstrating the importance of social support in maintaining a balanced nervous system.

Prolonged isolation can trigger the body's stress response, leading to a cycle of loneliness and poor vagal function. Engaging in social activities, even virtually, and fostering relationships can help activate the vagus nerve and improve emotional resilience.

Chapter 2 Summary

These factors can disrupt the vagus nerve's ability to function effectively, impacting both physical and mental health. Recognizing these signs can guide efforts to restore vagal tone and promote overall well-being.

- **Signs of poor vagal tone:**
  - chronic digestive issues such as constipation, bloating, and irregular bowel movements.
  - low stomach acid levels and poor nutrient absorption leading to fatigue and deficiencies.
  - connections to inflammatory conditions like IBS
- **Mental health symptoms:**
  - persistent anxiety, mood swings, and difficulty recovering from stress
  - heightened irritability and emotional sensitivity
- **Emotional and behavioral patterns:**
  - engagement in self-sabotaging habits and destructive coping mechanisms
  - difficulty maintaining calm and focus; emotional reactivity
  - social withdrawal and struggles with regulating emotions
- **Root causes of vagus nerve dysfunction:**
  - Chronic stress and trauma: Long-term stress impacts, trauma-induced hyperarousal, and lasting effects on the nervous system.
  - Harmful lifestyle choices: Poor diet, lack of exercise, inadequate sleep, and substance use negatively affect vagal tone.
  - Modern-day stressors: Overuse of technology and blue light screens, exposure to environmental toxins, and social stressors such as isolation.

Up next, "Chapter 3: Holistic Strategies to Energize Vagal Tone and Soften Anxiety," activating your internal calming and taking control of your mind, body, and balance.

HOLISTIC STRATEGIES TO ENERGIZE VAGAL TONE AND ADDRESS THE ROOT CAUSES OF SHAME

Discover how to activate your internal "calming switch" on a day-to-day basis with simple yet effective techniques for balanced, peaceful living.

Mindful Breathwork: The Foundation of Healing

The simple act of intentional breathing can have profound impacts on the nervous system, mental well-being, and the gut-brain connection. By focusing on breathwork, individuals can activate the vagus nerve and promote the parasympathetic response, which calms the body and mind. This section explores effective breath awareness techniques, their benefits, and how they can be practiced consistently for optimal results.

Breath Awareness for Cultivating Inner Peace

Breath awareness exercises can enhance the connection between the body and mind, creating a sense of inner peace. Here are three of the most effective and popular techniques:

Visualized Box Breathing

Box breathing, or four-square breathing, is a simple technique that promotes relaxation and mental focus. It is also called Navy breathing, attributed to the SEALs for calm during missions, and involves the following steps:

- **Inhale** for a count of four seconds, visualizing the first side of a box being drawn.
- **Hold your breath** for a count of four seconds as you picture the top of the box forming.
- **Exhale** slowly for a count of four seconds, visualizing the third side.
- **Hold your breath again** for a count of four seconds to complete the final side of the box.

Repeating this four-step cycle for several minutes activates the parasympathetic nervous system, enhancing vagal tone and reducing anxiety and feelings of shame (Grossman et al., 2004). The visualization aspect can help keep the mind engaged, which is especially helpful for individuals with racing thoughts.

Lion's Breath

Lion's breath is a more dynamic breath technique that releases tension and activates the vagus nerve through deep, powerful exhalations. It is practiced as follows:

- Sit comfortably with your hands on your knees.
- Inhale deeply through the nose.
- Open your mouth wide, stick out your tongue, and exhale forcefully while making an extended "haaaa" sound.

Lion's breath helps relieve tension in the jaw and face while promoting relaxation. The exaggerated breath engages the diaphragm and throat muscles, stimulating the vagus nerve and promoting a calming effect (Jerath et al., 2006).

Physiological Sigh

The physiological sigh is a double inhale followed by a long, slow exhale. It is especially effective when feeling overwhelmed or panicky. To perform this:

- Inhale deeply through the nose. Pause for a moment.
- Take a second, shorter inhale to fully expand the lungs.
- Exhale slowly through the mouth, extending the breath out for as long as possible.

This technique stimulates the parasympathetic nervous system by activating the vagus nerve, reducing the heart rate, and promoting relaxation. The physiological sigh has been shown to reduce anxiety and lower cortisol levels, which are key for managing stress (Huberman, 2021).

Benefits for Mind–Gut Connection

Breath awareness directly impacts the mind–gut connection. The vagus nerve, which plays a significant role in connecting the brain and gut, is influenced by the rhythm of breathing. Deep, controlled breathing helps signal the gut to maintain optimal mobility and balance. When practiced regularly, these breathing exercises can aid digestion and reduce symptoms of conditions like IBS by promoting a relaxed gut environment (Bonaz et al., 2018).

Effectiveness for Reducing Cortisol

Chronic stress leads to elevated cortisol levels, which can disrupt both mental and physical health. Regular breathwork practices have been shown to reduce cortisol, facilitating a return to homeostasis. Box breathing and the physiological sigh, in particular, help activate the vagus nerve, which signals the body to lower stress hormone production (Thayer & Sternberg, 2006). Reduced cortisol levels not only improve mental well-being but also benefit digestive health, as high cortisol can impair gut function.

Diaphragmatic Breathing Techniques

Diaphragmatic, or deep belly breathing, is one of the more effective techniques for stimulating the vagus nerve and promoting relaxation. This method enhances the body's ability to switch from the sympathetic "fight or flight" state to the parasympathetic "rest and digest" state.

Step-by-Step on Deep Breathing

- **Find a comfortable position**, either sitting or lying down.
- **Place one hand** on your chest and the other on your abdomen to feel the breath move.
- **Inhale deeply** through your nose, allowing your abdomen to rise while keeping your chest as still as possible.
- **Hold your breath** for a moment.
- **Exhale slowly** through your mouth, engaging your diaphragm to push the air out.
- **Extend the exhale** for as long as possible, ideally twice as long as the inhale, to activate the vagus nerve.

How It Stimulates the Vagus Nerve

Diaphragmatic breathing stimulates the vagus nerve by engaging the diaphragm, which is connected to this vital nerve. The long, controlled exhalations encourage vagal tone and signal the body to reduce heart rate and promote relaxation (Jerath et al., 2006). This practice has been shown to reduce symptoms of anxiety and improve HRV, an indicator of balanced nervous system function (Laborde et al., 2017).

Tips for Consistent Practice

- **Start small**, practicing for five minutes a day, and gradually increase the duration as it becomes more comfortable.
- **Incorporate breathing exercises into daily routines**, such as during a break at work or before bedtime.
- **Set reminders** or use a meditation app to stay consistent and track progress.

Alternate Nostril Breathing

Alternate nostril breathing, or *Nadi Shodhana*, is a yogic practice that balances the body's energy and regulates the nervous system.

How It Enhances Mental Clarity

This technique enhances mental clarity by promoting balanced oxygen flow to the brain, reducing stress, and calming the mind. Alternating the flow of breath between the nostrils harmonizes the left and right hemispheres of the brain, leading to improved focus and emotional stability (Telles et al., 2013).

Regulates the Nervous System

Alternate nostril breathing engages the parasympathetic nervous system, reducing stress and promoting a state of calm. The rhythmic nature of this practice helps balance the autonomic nervous system and improve vagal tone, contributing to a relaxed state that supports mental and digestive health (Zope & Zope, 2013).

Best Practices for Effective Results

- **Sit comfortably** with your spine straight and eyes closed.
- **Use your thumb** to close the right nostril and inhale deeply through the left nostril.
- **Close the left nostril** with your ring finger, open the right nostril, and exhale fully.
- **Inhale through the right nostril**, close it with your thumb, and open the left nostril to exhale.
- **Repeat the cycle** for 5–10 minutes, focusing on slow, even breaths.

Regular practice of alternate nostril breathing can improve resilience to stress and enhance cognitive function by stimulating the vagus nerve and balancing the autonomic nervous system (Jerath et al., 2006).

Meditation to Lower the Volume of Self-Defeating Mental Chatter

Meditation has long been recognized for its transformative power in fostering mental clarity and emotional resilience. One of its most significant benefits is its effect on the vagus nerve, which, as we've discussed, plays a pivotal role in regulating the parasympathetic nervous system. By practicing meditation, individuals can employ a less physical approach to enhance their vagal tone, leading to improved anxiety management and a reduction in negative, self-defeating mental chatter.

This section will explore the science behind meditation's benefits, practical mindfulness techniques, and specific exercises like ASMR and progressive muscle relaxation (PMR) that can be easily integrated into daily routines.

How Meditation Re-Connects You to Your Vagus Nerve

The Science Behind Meditation's Benefits

Meditation influences the autonomic nervous system by stimulating the vagus nerve and promoting parasympathetic activity. Research shows that regular meditation practice can enhance HRV, an indicator of good vagal tone, which in turn leads to better stress management and emotional regulation (Gerritsen & Band, 2018). The calming nature of meditation encourages the release of neurotransmitters like serotonin and dopamine, fostering a sense of well-being and mental clarity (Wielgosz et al., 2019).

Functional MRI scans have demonstrated that meditation reduces activity in the amygdala—the brain's fear and emotional center—and increases connectivity in areas associated with executive function and emotional regulation. This shift helps manage the fight or flight response, allowing the body to return to a state of calm more effectively (Taren et al., 2015).

Simple Ways to Integrate Meditation Into Your Routine

Incorporating meditation doesn't require hours of practice each day. Here are some simple ways to include meditation in daily life:

- **Morning routine:** Dedicate 5–10 minutes upon waking for a short meditation session to set a peaceful tone for the day.
- **Guided meditation apps:** Use apps such as Headspace or Calm to follow guided meditations that specifically focus on stress reduction and vagus nerve stimulation.
- **Breath-focused meditation:** Close your eyes and focus solely on the breath. Observe each inhale and exhale, extending the breath out for as long as possible to activate the vagus nerve. Concentrating on your breaths will distract you from interruptive thoughts.

How Meditation Aids Anxiety Relief

Regular meditation practice aids in reducing anxiety by enhancing vagal tone and promoting the body's parasympathetic state. When the vagus nerve is activated, it helps to lower cortisol levels, decrease heart rate, and reduce overall stress response. This physiological shift promotes a state of relaxation, allowing individuals to detach from self-defeating thoughts and foster resilience (Thayer & Lane, 2009).

Practical Mindfulness Techniques and Guided Visualization Exercises

Mindfulness Techniques

Mindfulness involves paying attention to the present moment without judgment. This practice can be enhanced through various techniques:

- **Body scan meditation:** Slowly move your awareness through each part of your body, starting from your toes and working up to your head. This technique promotes bodily awareness and helps release tension, which can activate the vagus nerve (Kabat-Zinn, 2013).
- **Gratitude meditation:** Focus on things you are grateful for and visualize them in your mind. This practice can shift focus away from negative mental chatter and reduce stress by stimulating positive emotional responses.

Guided Visualization Exercises

Guided visualization is a form of meditation that uses mental imagery to promote relaxation and well-being. A simple exercise could involve imagining yourself in a serene setting, such as a forest or beach, where you feel safe and calm. This visualization encourages the brain to produce calming neurotransmitters and reduces the activity of stress-inducing pathways (Wielgosz et al., 2019).

To practice:

- Sit comfortably and close your eyes.
- Visualize yourself in a peaceful environment.

- Engage your senses by imagining the sounds, smells, and textures around you.
- Breathe deeply, allowing your body to relax as you immerse yourself in the visualization.

Autonomous Sensory Meridian Response

What Is ASMR?

Autonomous sensory meridian response (ASMR) refers to the tingling sensation some people experience when exposed to specific auditory and visual stimuli, such as whispering, tapping, or soft scratching. ASMR videos and audio recordings have gained popularity as tools for relaxation and anxiety relief. The slow-paced and gentle nature of these sounds helps activate the parasympathetic nervous system, promoting a state of calm that can enhance vagal tone (Poerio et al., 2018).

How ASMR Reduces Heart Rate and Calms the Mind

Studies have shown that ASMR can reduce heart rate and increase feelings of relaxation. The experience activates regions of the brain associated with reward and emotional arousal, such as the nucleus accumbens and the prefrontal cortex (Barratt & Davis, 2015). These changes can help soothe anxiety, interrupt self-defeating thought patterns, and promote a sense of well-being.

Simple Ways to Integrate ASMR Into Your Routine

- **Listen before bed:** Use ASMR recordings as part of a bedtime routine to signal the body to enter a parasympathetic state, facilitating sleep.
- **Take a break:** Listen to ASMR during short breaks

throughout the day to recharge and manage stress levels.

- **Experiment with different triggers:** ASMR is highly individual, so experiment with different sounds to find what works best for you.

Progressive Muscle Relaxation

Releasing Tension Stored in Muscles

PMR is a relaxation technique that involves systematically tensing and then releasing different muscle groups in the body. This practice helps release stored tension, reduce muscle fatigue, and activate the vagus nerve, contributing to enhanced parasympathetic activity (McCallie et al., 2006).

5–10 Minute Daily Guided Practices

PMR can be practiced in as little as 5–10 minutes each day. Here's a step-by-step guide:

- **Find a quiet space** where you won't be disturbed.
- **Close your eyes** and take a few deep breaths.
- **Start with your feet.** Tense the muscles in your feet for 5–7 seconds, then release.
- **Move up the body.** Progressively tense and release the calves, thighs, abdomen, chest, arms, and finally, the face.
- **Focus on the feeling** of relaxation after each release, noting how your body feels as tension melts away.

Systematic Body Relaxation

By systematically tensing and relaxing muscles, PMR helps activate the vagus nerve and improve vagal tone. This practice shifts the body into a state of relaxation, reducing stress and promoting calm (Conrad & Roth, 2007). Consistent practice of PMR can also aid in better sleep, reduced anxiety, and overall mental well-being.

Impact on Vagal Tone

PMR enhances vagal tone by promoting relaxation and reducing heart rate. When practiced regularly, it can increase HRV, indicating a stronger vagal response and better stress resilience (Lehrer & Gevirtz, 2014). This improvement contributes to emotional stability and a more balanced nervous system, aiding in the management of anxiety and intrusive mental chatter.

Lifestyle Habits for Lasting Serenity

The foundation for a balanced nervous system and improved vagal tone lies in holistic lifestyle habits. These habits support not just the body but also the mind, contributing to long-term serenity. This section will cover daily movement and gentle exercise, improving sleep quality, and the calming effects of connecting with nature. Each practice plays a role in energizing vagal tone, supporting relaxation, and maintaining mental and physical health.

Daily Movement and Gentle Exercise

How Gentle Movement Aids the Nervous System

Gentle movement is essential for supporting the nervous system and promoting relaxation, particularly after consuming a large meal. Physical activity stimulates the vagus nerve, which helps activate the parasympathetic "rest and digest" response. Gentle exercise, such as walking or stretching, can enhance gut motility and reduce bloating by promoting the movement of food through the digestive system. This, in turn, helps reduce stress on the body and fosters a sense of calm.

Regular movement also increases HRV, a sign of good vagal tone and nervous system health. Activities that focus on slow, controlled movement, such as yoga or tai chi, are especially effective in stimulating the vagus nerve and calming the mind (Ross & Thomas, 2010).

Intro to Yoga, Walking, and Stretching

- **Yoga:** A practice that combines gentle movements, controlled breathing, and meditation, yoga has been shown to increase vagal tone and reduce stress. Specific poses, like the forward bend, cat-cow, cobra, downward-facing dog, and the child's pose, can be particularly calming. (More about yoga practice coming up in Chapter 5.)
- **Walking:** A simple yet effective way to stimulate the vagus nerve and improve mental health. Walking, especially in nature, helps decrease stress hormones and improve mood (Marselle et al., 2019).
- **Stretching:** Engaging in light stretching before or after meals can promote relaxation by releasing

muscle tension and enhancing circulation. But avoid bending exercises after eating to avoid indigestion!

Incorporating Movement Into Your Lifestyle

- **Morning routine:** Start your day with 10–15 minutes of gentle stretching or a brief yoga session to awaken your body and stimulate the vagus nerve.
- **Post-meal walks:** Incorporate short, 10–15 minute walks after meals to aid digestion and reduce post-meal fatigue. But take it slow after eating.
- **Mindful movement breaks:** Schedule short breaks throughout the day to practice stretching or engage in simple exercises to maintain energy and reduce stress. Even getting up out of a sitting position for 10 to 15 minutes is beneficial.

Improving Sleep Quality

Sleep's Effect on the Nervous System

Sleep plays an integral role in maintaining nervous system health. During sleep, the body engages in repair processes that strengthen the immune system, consolidate memories, and regulate emotional responses. Quality sleep is essential for healthy serotonin and melatonin production. Serotonin, produced during the day, is a precursor to melatonin, which helps regulate the sleep-wake cycle (Gao et al., 2017). Good sleep improves vagal tone, supporting better stress management and emotional stability.

Tips for Deep, Restorative Sleep

- **Sunlight exposure:** Start your day with 15–30 minutes of natural sunlight exposure to signal to your body that it's time to be alert. Sunlight helps regulate your internal body clock, known as the circadian rhythm, and promotes serotonin production, which eventually converts to melatonin at night (Wright et al., 2013).
- **Consistent sleep schedule:** Go to bed and wake up at the same time every day, even on weekends. This consistency reinforces the body's natural circadian rhythm, making it easier to fall and stay asleep.
- **Before bedtime:** Avoid coffee, tea, and other caffeinated beverages, and don't have alcohol close to bedtime.
- **Sleep environment:** Ensure your bedroom is dark, cool, and quiet. Blackout curtains, a white noise machine, and a comfortable mattress can all contribute to better sleep quality.

Non-Sleep Deep Rest

Non-sleep deep rest (NSDR) refers to techniques that promote a state of deep relaxation without actual sleep. This includes practices like yoga nidra or guided meditation. NSDR helps reduce stress, improve focus, and enhance the parasympathetic response, supporting vagal tone (Summer & Peters., (2024, February 26). Incorporating NSDR into your daily routine can act as a midday reset, allowing you to manage stress more effectively and sleep more soundly at night.

How to Practice NSDR

- **Find a comfortable** space where you can lie down or sit in a reclined position.
- **Close your eyes** and focus on your breath, gradually relaxing each part of your body.
- **Listen** to a guided NSDR practice or simply visualize calming imagery, focusing on the release of tension and deep relaxation.

Connecting With Nature

Nature's Impact on Mental Calm

Connecting with nature is a surprisingly effective way to boost mental well-being and reduce stress. Spending time in green spaces has been shown to lower cortisol levels and improve mood, contributing to an overall sense of peace (Hartig et al., 2014). Nature exposure also enhances vagal tone by encouraging slower, deeper breathing and relaxation, which supports the activation of the parasympathetic nervous system (Berman et al., 2012).

Grounding, or earthing, is a specific practice that involves direct contact with the earth, such as walking barefoot on grass or sand. This contact can help neutralize free radicals in the body, reducing inflammation and promoting calm.

Strategies for Grounding and Earthing

- **Morning walks:** Start your day with a walk in a nearby park or nature trail to set a calming tone.
- **Barefoot time:** Spend a few minutes each day

standing or walking barefoot on natural surfaces like grass, sand, or soil.

- **Garden time:** If possible, cultivate a small garden or spend time caring for plants to deepen your connection with nature.

How to Make It a Regular Practice

- **Set a routine:** Schedule time for nature walks or grounding exercises, even if only for 10–15 minutes a day.
- **Combine with meditation:** Practice mindfulness during your time in nature by focusing on the sounds, sights, and sensations around you.
- **Bring nature indoors:** For days when going outside isn't possible, bring nature into your home with indoor plants or a small water feature to create a calming environment. Even apartment dwellers can cultivate and care for indoor plants.

Chapter 3 Summary

Each of these holistic strategies supports a balanced nervous system, enhancing vagal tone and promoting overall well-being:

- **Breath awareness for inner peace:**
  - techniques include visualized box breathing, lion's breath, and the physiological sigh
  - benefits shown for mind–gut connection and cortisol reduction
  - step-by-step guides and tips for consistent practice
- **Diaphragmatic breathing techniques:**
  - how deep breathing stimulates the vagus nerve

- o step-by-step instructions and benefits for extending exhalations
- o tips for integrating into daily life
- **Alternate nostril breathing:**
  - o enhances mental clarity and balances the nervous system
  - o best practices for effective results
- **Meditation to lower self-defeating mental chatter:**
  - o meditation's impact on the vagus nerve and anxiety relief
  - o mindfulness and guided visualization exercises
  - o introduction to ASMR for relaxation and vagal tone
  - o PMR for systematic body relaxation
- **Lifestyle habits for lasting serenity:**
  - o benefits of daily movement like yoga and walking for nervous system health
  - o importance of sleep quality and practices for restorative sleep, including NSDR
  - o connecting with nature to boost mental calm and how to make it a regular habit

You are what you eat! "Chapter 4: Dietary Choices for a Harmonized Gut and Optimal Vagal Activation" discusses the nutritional aspects of the gut-brain connection. Yes, your diet can impact your mental clarity as well as your physical condition.

DIETARY CHOICES FOR A HARMONIZED GUT AND OPTIMAL VAGAL ACTIVATION

Nourish your gut for greater moments of mental clarity: Let's discuss the gut–brain connection! Discover how proper nutrition can strengthen the impact of the vagus nerve.

Foods to Support Vagal Tone and Mental Focus

The relationship between diet and nervous system health is profound. The right dietary choices can enhance vagal tone, support mental clarity, and nurture overall well-being, helping to reduce the risks of diseases ranging from heart disease and type 2 diabetes to cancer. This section explores specific anti-inflammatory foods, healthy fats, and nutrients that play a vital role in optimizing vagal activation and mental focus.

Anti-Inflammatory Foods

A diet that reduces inflammation is crucial for maintaining a balanced gut–brain connection and stimulating the vagus nerve. Chronic inflammation can impair the vagus nerve's ability to regulate the parasympathetic response, making it harder for the body to manage stress and promote healing (Calder, 2017). Emphasizing an organic, plant-based diet can help manage inflammation and support overall health.

Omega-3-Rich Foods

Omega-3 fatty acids are essential for brain health and play a significant role in reducing inflammation. They support the structure and function of neurons, enhance cognitive performance, and help regulate mood. Sources of plant-based omega-3s include:

- **Chia seeds:** High in alpha-linolenic acid (ALA), chia seeds are an excellent addition to smoothies, oatmeal, or salads.
- **Flaxseeds:** Ground flaxseeds provide a boost of ALA and can be incorporated into baked goods or sprinkled over breakfast bowls.
- **Pumpkin seeds and raw nuts:** Rich in both omega-3s and other beneficial nutrients, nuts and seeds support brain health and reduce inflammation (Swanson et al., 2012).
- **Organic avocados:** Packed with healthy fats and antioxidants, avocados contribute to cognitive function and a reduction in systemic inflammation.

For those whose diet is low in seafood, algae-based supplements can be an alternative source of DHA and EPA, forms of omega-3s that are crucial for brain and nervous system health.

Turmeric, Ginger, and Other Anti-Inflammatory Spices

Natural spices are not only flavorful but also powerful anti-inflammatories. Incorporating spices such as **turmeric** (containing curcumin), **ginger**, **cloves**, and **ceylon cinnamon** into meals and beverages can help modulate inflammation and support vagal tone (Hewlings & Kalman, 2017).

- **Turmeric and curcumin:** Curcumin has been shown to reduce inflammation and oxidative stress, which can positively impact brain health and the function of the vagus nerve.
- **Ginger:** Known for its anti-inflammatory and digestive benefits, ginger can be consumed as a tea or added to stir-fries and smoothies.
- **Cinnamon and cloves:** These spices possess antioxidants that help combat inflammation and protect the nervous system.

Drinking herbal teas that include these spices can also be a soothing way to support vagal tone throughout the day.

Benefits of Reducing Inflammation on Vagal Tone

Lowering inflammation reduces strain on the body's nervous system. This improvement in systemic health allows the vagus nerve to perform its role in regulating heart rate, digestion, and relaxation more effectively. A diet rich in anti-inflammatory foods has been associated with better autonomic balance and improved stress response (Calder, 2017).

Healthy Fats and Vagal Tone

Healthy fats are essential for optimal brain function, mental clarity, and maintaining a well-regulated nervous system. Unlike saturated and trans fats, which can contribute to inflammation, healthy fats support the body's production of cell membranes and neurotransmitters.

Benefits of Avocados, Nuts, Seeds, and Cold-Pressed Olive Oil

- **Avocados:** Full of monounsaturated fats, avocados help maintain healthy blood flow to the brain and support cognitive function. They also contain vitamin E, which acts as an antioxidant to protect brain cells from oxidative stress.
- **Nuts and seeds:** Almonds, walnuts, and pumpkin seeds are not only sources of omega-3s but also provide magnesium and B vitamins, which are critical for nervous system health.
- **Whole Olives or Organic Cold-Pressed EVOO:** Rich in polyphenols and monounsaturated fats, olive oil has anti-inflammatory properties that support brain health and may enhance vagal tone by reducing inflammation (Visioli & Galli, 2002).

The Role of Fats in Mental Clarity and Brain Health

Healthy fats contribute to the myelination of neurons (formation of the protective, insulating sheath that coats the long nerve axons), which speeds up signal transmission and supports cognitive processes. Diets rich in healthy fats have been linked to better memory retention and reduced risk of cognitive decline (Gómez-Pinilla, 2008). These benefits are amplified when healthy fats are combined with nutrient-dense, non-starchy vegetables such as leafy greens and cruciferous vegetables, which provide essential vitamins and minerals.

How to Add Healthy Fats Without Extra Calories

To incorporate healthy fats while maintaining a balanced diet, consider the following:

- Use **avocado slices** as a spread or in salads.
- Add **small portions of raw nuts** to snacks or meals.
- Drizzle **cold-pressed olive oil** over steamed vegetables or salads.

Avoid combining these fats with refined carbohydrates or sugars, as this combination can lead to weight gain and metabolic issues. Instead, pair healthy fats with leafy greens and non-starchy vegetables to maximize nutrient absorption and satiety (feeling full).

Nervous System-Nurturing Nutrients

Specific nutrients are vital for the health and function of the nervous system, directly impacting vagal tone and mental focus.

Foods High in Magnesium

Magnesium is crucial for muscle relaxation, neurotransmitter function, and overall nervous system health. It can help regulate the body's response to stress by supporting the function of the parasympathetic nervous system.

- **Leafy Greens:** Greens such as spinach, collard greens and kale are rich in magnesium and can be included in salads or smoothies.
- **Nuts and beans:** Almonds, black and pinto beans, and chickpeas are excellent sources of magnesium that also provide protein and fiber.
- **Dark Chocolate (at least 70%; up to 85% cocoa):** Low in sugar and contains magnesium and

antioxidants, which help reduce stress and support brain health.

Vitamin B-Rich Foods for Nervous System Function

B vitamins, especially B1, B6, B9 (folate), and B12, are essential for neurotransmitter production and energy metabolism. These vitamins help regulate mood and enhance mental clarity.

- **Whole Grains**, **Legumes** (beans, chickpeas, lentils), and **leafy greens** are abundant in B vitamins that contribute to nervous system health.
- **Nutritional Yeast** can be sprinkled over dishes as a source of B vitamins (particularly B12) and protein.
- **Tofu or Tempeh** is an excellent source of protein as it contains all 8 essential amino acids, magnesium, zinc, and vitamin B1 (thiamine).

Hydration's Role in Nervous System Balance

Staying hydrated is essential for optimal nervous system and bodily function. Water accounts for an average of 60% of body mass, supports the transport of nutrients, aids in digestion, and helps regulate body temperature. Dehydration can lead to increased cortisol levels and impaired cognitive function, impacting mood and stress response (Popkin et al., 2010).

Tips for Ensuring Adequate Hydration:

- Drink at least **10-12 glasses of water** or water-based beverages daily, depending on activity level and climate.
- Start the day with a glass of water to kickstart metabolism and rehydrate after sleep.

- Infuse water with **citrus slices** or mint for added flavor and a nutritional boost.

Gut-Brain Superfoods to Support Anxious Energy and Digestive Health

As noted, the food we consume plays a crucial role in the health of our gut microbiome and its connection to the brain. Incorporating *gut-friendly superfoods* like fermented vegetables, probiotics, prebiotics, and calming herbs can significantly support anxious energy and enhance digestive health. This section explores how these specific foods contribute to the gut–brain axis and offers practical ways to integrate them into your daily routine.

The Role of Fermented Foods and Probiotics

How Fermented Foods Support the Gut Microbiome

Fermented foods are rich in probiotics, which are beneficial bacteria that support the gut microbiome. A balanced gut microbiome is essential for the production of neurotransmitters like serotonin, which impacts mood and mental health. Approximately 90% of serotonin is produced in the gut, underscoring the gut's influence on emotional well-being (Clapp et al., 2017). Probiotics from fermented foods can help maintain a diverse and balanced microbial population, promoting optimal gut health and vagal tone.

Benefits of Probiotic Foods

Incorporating fermented foods into your diet can provide a natural boost to gut health and anxiety management. Here are some excellent sources of probiotics:

- **Pickled Vegetables:** Fermented cucumbers, carrots, and other pickled veggies are rich in live cultures that support digestion.
- **Sauerkraut and Kimchi:** These fermented cabbage dishes are packed with probiotics and vitamins that aid digestion and promote gut health.
- **Kombucha:** A fermented tea rich in probiotics, kombucha can support digestion and provide a refreshing alternative to sugary drinks.
- **Tempeh and Miso:** Fermented soy products like tempeh and miso are not only rich in probiotics but also contain protein and essential nutrients that promote gut health.
- **Natto:** A traditional Japanese dish made from fermented soybeans, natto is an excellent source of probiotics and vitamin K2, supporting both gut and cardiovascular health (Ouwehand et al., 2010).

Tips for Daily Incorporation

- **Start small:** If you're new to fermented foods, introduce them gradually to allow your gut to adapt. Start with a small serving of sauerkraut or a half-cup of kombucha and increase over time.
- **Diversify:** Rotate different types of fermented foods to maximize exposure to various strains of beneficial bacteria.
- **Pair with meals:** Add a spoonful of sauerkraut or kimchi to salads, sandwiches, or grain bowls for a tangy, gut-friendly boost.

Prebiotics That Feed Gut Bacteria

While **pro**biotics introduce billions of beneficial bacteria, **pre**biotics are non-digestible fibers that serve as food for these microbes in the intestines, helping them thrive. Incorporating prebiotics into your diet supports a robust gut microbiome.

Examples of Prebiotic Foods

- **Fruits:** Bananas, apples, and berries are excellent sources of prebiotic fibers like pectin. Papaya, kiwi, mango, and pineapple offer an excellent array of digestive enzymes to assist with digestion and the absorption of nutrients.
- **Vegetables:** Garlic, onions, leeks, and asparagus are particularly high in prebiotic fibers that fuel gut bacteria.
- **Legumes and Whole Grains:** Lentils, beans, chickpeas, oats, and barley provide complex carbohydrates that support gut health.
- **Nuts and Seeds:** Almonds, flaxseeds, and chia seeds are nutrient-dense and contain fibers that promote the growth of healthy gut bacteria (Slavin, 2013).

Incorporation Tips

- **Mix fruits and seeds:** Create a breakfast bowl with bananas, ground flaxseeds, and a drizzle of almond butter.
- **Add vegetables:** Incorporate garlic and onions into stir-fries or soups for an easy prebiotic boost. Health tip: half your plate should include stir-fried, boiled or roasted veggies or a fresh salad.

- **Snacks and salads:** Sprinkle prebiotic-rich seeds over salads or use them in homemade energy bars.

Herbs and Teas for Calming Effects

Herbal teas have been used for centuries to promote relaxation and improve overall well-being. Many herbs contain compounds that can reduce inflammation and support the parasympathetic nervous system, enhancing vagal tone and promoting calm.

Chamomile, Lavender, and Hibiscus

- **Chamomile:** Known for its calming properties, chamomile contains antioxidants like apigenin, which binds to certain brain receptors and promotes relaxation (Srivastava et al., 2010). Drinking chamomile tea before bed can enhance sleep quality and support stress reduction.
- **Lavender:** Often associated with relaxation, lavender contains linalool, a compound that helps reduce anxiety and promote a sense of calm (Koulivand et al., 2013). Sipping on lavender tea or adding a few drops of food-grade lavender oil to warm water can be soothing.
- **Hibiscus:** High in antioxidants, hibiscus tea helps reduce inflammation and support cardiovascular health, which indirectly benefits vagal tone and stress management.

Herbal Tea: Simple Recipes for Daily Calm

Today, there are many alternatives to herbal teas in specialty stores and even in most supermarkets. Many should be served simply or as a mix of herbs:

- **Chamomile and Lavender Blend:**
    - Steep 1 teaspoon of dried chamomile flowers and 1/2 teaspoon of dried lavender in hot water for 5–7 minutes.
    - Strain and enjoy as a soothing evening drink.
- **Hibiscus and Mint Cooler:**
    - Steep 1 teaspoon of dried hibiscus petals in hot water for 5 minutes.
    - Add a few fresh mint leaves and allow the tea to cool. Serve over ice for a refreshing and calming beverage.

Green Tea Instead of Coffee

Green tea is a great alternative to coffee for those looking to reduce anxiety. It contains **L-theanine**, an amino acid known for promoting relaxation without drowsiness. L-theanine enhances alpha brain waves, which are associated with a calm but alert state, and supports the production of neurotransmitters that reduce stress (Unno et al., 2018). Additionally, green tea has anti-inflammatory properties that benefit both the gut and the brain. You can enjoy green tea plain, without adding anything, or consider this variation:

- **Green tea with Lemon Balm:**
    - Brew a cup of green tea and add a few lemon balm leaves or a drop of lemon balm extract.
    - Sip in the morning or mid-afternoon for a gentle energy boost without the jitters of coffee that some people experience.

Foods to Avoid for Optimal Nervous System Health

Maintaining a balanced diet that supports the gut-brain axis and promotes optimal vagal tone requires not just adding nutritious foods but also avoiding certain harmful substances, many of which are commonly available: Processed foods, refined sugars, stimulants, and artificial additives can all negatively impact the nervous system, impair gut health, and exacerbate anxiety. This section delves into why these food categories should be limited or avoided and offers practical advice for transitioning to a cleaner, nervous system-friendly diet.

Processed Foods and Refined Sugars (Sucrose, Fructose)

Negative Impact on Gut Health and Anxiety

Processed foods and refined sugars have been shown to negatively impact gut health by promoting inflammation and disrupting the balance of the gut microbiome. High levels of refined sugars, such as sucrose and high-fructose corn syrup, can lead to the proliferation of harmful gut bacteria and the reduction of beneficial strains. This imbalance can trigger systemic inflammation and interfere with the production of essential neurotransmitters, such as serotonin, which is critical for mood regulation (Khanna et al., 2018).

Refined sugars can also contribute to blood sugar spikes and crashes, leading to mood swings, irritability, and increased anxiety. The resulting metabolic fluctuations can exacerbate stress responses and impair the parasympathetic nervous system's ability to maintain balance, thus negatively affecting the vagal tone (Jia & Wardak, 2022).

How Processed Foods Affect Vagal Tone

The vagus nerve, as previously explained, plays a pivotal role in promoting the "rest and digest" response. Processed foods are often low in fiber and high in unhealthy fats, refined sugars, and additives, which can impair gut motility and digestion. These foods promote inflammation, which can weaken vagal tone over time. In contrast, a diet rich in whole, nutrient-dense foods supports vagus nerve activation and improves overall nervous system function (Breit et al., 2018).

Practical Tips to Reduce Processed Sugar Intake

- **Read labels:** Become familiar with the various names of added sugars, such as high-fructose corn syrup, maltose, and dextrose, and limit products containing these ingredients. Honey, maple syrup, and "sugar in the raw" are no different nutritionally than processed white table sugar.
- **Choose natural sweeteners:** Use natural sweeteners like stevia, but do so in moderation.
- **Prioritize whole foods:** Prepare meals using fresh, whole ingredients to control sugar intake and support your gut microbiome.
- **Opt for fruit:** Satisfy your sweet cravings with fruits, which provide fiber and vitamins along with natural sugars. Tip: Frozen fruit is ideal for smoothies or can be quickly thawed by placing it in a glass or ceramic bowl and pouring boiled water on top. Let sit for 2-3 minutes before draining.

Stimulants and Their Effects

Effects of Caffeine and Alcohol on the Nervous System

Caffeine and alcohol are two common stimulants that can disrupt the nervous system when consumed in excess. While moderate caffeine consumption can have cognitive benefits, excessive intake can overstimulate the nervous system, leading to increased anxiety, jitteriness, and sleep disturbances. Caffeine consumption can also trigger the release of cortisol, the stress hormone, which, when chronically elevated, impairs the body's ability to engage the calming parasympathetic response (Lovallo et al., 2005).

Alcohol, on the other hand, can initially act as a depressant and cause sleepiness but later disrupts sleep and impairs vagal tone. Chronic alcohol use can lead to changes in gut permeability, promoting inflammation and negatively affecting the gut-brain axis. These disruptions can impair the vagus nerve's function, making it more difficult for the body to recover from stress and maintain emotional stability (Bishehsari et al., 2017).

Alternatives to Reduce Dependency on Stimulants

- **Caffeine-free herbal teas:** Chamomile, rooibos, and peppermint teas provide soothing, non-stimulating alternatives that can promote relaxation and support the nervous system.
- **Morning adaptogens:** Consider starting the day with adaptogenic drinks made from ashwagandha or holy basil, which help modulate the body's stress response without overstimulation.
- **Kombucha:** This probiotic-rich drink can offer a

slight energy boost with less caffeine than coffee, promoting gut health at the same time.

Healthy Substitutions for Coffee and Alcohol

- **Green tea** (see previous section) **or Matcha**: These beverages contain lower levels of caffeine than coffee and include **L-theanine**, an amino acid known for its calming effects and ability to enhance mental focus without causing jitters (Unno et al., 2018).
- **Mocktails with herbal infusions**: Swap alcoholic drinks for mocktails made with ingredients like ginger, lemon, and sparkling water infused with herbs for a calming, alcohol-free beverage. Mocktails taste like traditional spirits and cocktails but are alcohol-free.

Additives and Artificial Ingredients

How Additives Disrupt Gut Health

Artificial additives, such as preservatives, colorings, and flavor enhancers, can disrupt gut health by altering the composition of the gut microbiome and triggering inflammation. Studies have shown that certain food additives, like artificial sweeteners and emulsifiers, can negatively affect gut bacteria, leading to imbalances that promote metabolic dysfunction and increase the risk of mood disorders (Chassaing et al., 2015).

Artificial ingredients can impair the gut–brain axis by causing irritation and inflammation in the gut lining. This inflammation can weaken vagal tone and make the body more susceptible to anxiety and stress-related disorders (Bischoff, 2011).

Recognizing and Avoiding Common Additives

- **Read ingredient lists:** Be cautious of foods that contain long lists of unfamiliar ingredients, as these often include artificial additives.

- **Avoid artificial sweeteners:** Ingredients like aspartame, sucralose, and saccharin can negatively impact gut health and should be limited. Stevia, in contrast, is a natural plant extract.

- **Minimize packaged foods:** Packaged and processed foods are more likely to contain additives and preservatives. Choose fresh or minimally processed alternatives whenever possible.

- Steps to Transition to a Cleaner Diet

- **Cook at home:** Preparing meals at home gives you full control over the ingredients used, allowing you to avoid additives and artificial substances.

- **Choose organic when possible:** Organic foods are less likely to contain synthetic additives like glyphosate and other pesticides that can disrupt gut health.

- **Start small:** Gradually swap processed foods with whole, nutrient-dense options like fresh fruits, vegetables, whole grains, beans, nuts, and seeds.

- **Hydrate with water:** Limit sodas (which are loaded with sugar or high-fructose corn syrup) and artificial drinks, and stay hydrated with water or herbal teas to support digestion and overall nervous system health.

Chapter 4 Summary

Chapter 4 provides a comprehensive guide on which foods to include and avoid to support the gut–brain connection, promote vagal tone, and foster mental and digestive well-being.

- **Foods to support vagal tone and mental focus:**
    - emphasis on organic, plant-based diets rich in omega-3s (chia, flaxseeds, avocado, nuts) and anti-inflammatory spices (turmeric, clove, ginger, ceylon cinnamon)
    - outlines benefits of reducing inflammation to enhance vagal tone and overall brain health
- **Healthy fats and vagal tone**:
    - highlights the importance of avocados, nuts, seeds, and olives for brain function and mental clarity
    - tips for adding healthy fats without combining them with refined sugars or carbs
    - Encourages pairing fats with leafy greens and non-starchy vegetables.
- **Nervous system-nurturing nutrients:**
    - lists magnesium-rich foods (leafy greens, nuts, beans, dark chocolate) and vitamin B-rich foods (whole grains, legumes) for nervous system function
    - stresses the importance of hydration for optimal nervous system balance
- **Gut–brain superfoods for anxious energy and digestive health**:
    - covers fermented foods (sauerkraut, kimchi, kombucha) and their benefits for gut health and anxiety reduction

- o discusses prebiotic foods (fruits, vegetables, whole grains) that nourish gut bacteria
- o fruits high in digestive enzymes help accelerate overall digestion
- o recommends herbal teas like chamomile and green tea for calming effects
- **Foods to avoid for optimal nervous system health:**
  - o advises against processed foods and refined sugars due to their impact on gut health and vagal tone
  - o discusses the negative effects of stimulants (caffeine and alcohol) and offers healthier alternatives
  - o explains the disruptive nature of artificial additives and how to transition to a cleaner diet

Getting into good physical condition is one of the most important things to do for overall health. "Chapter 5: The Mastery Behind Movement: How a Basic Exercise Routine Can Significantly Enhance Vagal Tone" will explain why and how to shape up and stay fit.

THE MASTERY BEHIND MOVEMENT— HOW A BASIC EXERCISE ROUTINE CAN SIGNIFICANTLY ENHANCE VAGAL TONE

Did you know? Even simple movements such as 30 minutes of walking per day, taking the stairs instead of the elevator, or incorporating a brief afternoon stretch break can stimulate your vagus nerve to lessen the degree of anxiety symptoms.

Gentle Physical Activity for a Thriving Nervous System

Regular movement is essential for maintaining physical health and enhancing the function of the vagus nerve to promote relaxation and reduce stress. Gentle forms of exercise, such as walking, yoga, and stretching, can stimulate vagal tone, elevate mood, and improve overall mental clarity. This section explores how daily walks, yoga, and flexibility practices can contribute to a thriving nervous system. There are simple start-up descriptions of poses and stretches, but use the free online instructional videos on YouTube for a full range of exercises and their movements.

Daily Walks for Refreshing Your Mind

How Walking Stimulates Vagal Tone

Walking, particularly when done at a moderate pace, can stimulate the vagus nerve and activate the parasympathetic nervous system. The gentle, rhythmic motion of walking encourages deeper, controlled breathing, which is linked to enhanced vagal activity. This activation helps lower the heart rate, improve HRV, and reduce stress. Engaging the body in physical activity, such as walking, supports the vagus nerve's role in regulating the "rest and digest" response.

Benefits of Outdoor Walks on Mood

Walking outdoors provides additional benefits for mental health due to exposure to natural elements and sunlight. Sunlight exposure boosts serotonin levels, a neurotransmitter that contributes to mood stabilization and feelings of well-being (Young, 2007). Walking in green spaces has been shown to decrease cortisol levels and promote relaxation, making it an effective strategy for managing anxiety and boosting mood (Marselle et al., 2019).

Tips for Making Walking a Habit

- **Set a schedule:** Choose a consistent time each day, such as mornings or after dinner, to make walking part of your routine.
- **Start small:** If you have been sedentary and are out of shape, begin with 10-minute walks and gradually increase to 30 minutes or longer.
- **Moderate pacing:** There's no need to push too hard or too fast, especially if you are older. A

moderate pace that deepens your breathing is
sufficient.

- **Combine with mindfulness:** Pay attention to
  your surroundings, the rhythm of your steps, and your
  breathing to enhance the meditative effect of walking.
- **Track progress:** Use a pedometer or smartphone
  app to monitor steps and set achievable goals for
  motivation. Don't worry about reaching 10,000 steps
  a day; that comes from a marketing gimmick.
  Reaching 5,000 steps a day is both reachable and
  beneficial.

The Benefits of Yoga for Vagal Tone

Gentle Poses and Stretches That Stimulate the Vagus Nerve

Yoga is a highly effective practice for stimulating vagal tone and
promoting relaxation. Gentle poses that involve slow, deep
breathing and mindful stretching can engage the diaphragm
and stimulate the vagus nerve. For example, child's pose
(*Balasana*), cat-cow stretch (*Marjaryasana-Bitilasana*), cobra,
downward-facing dog, and legs up the wall (*Viparita Karani*)
are particularly beneficial. You can find instructive free
YouTube videos online; here are directions for these five beginner's poses and stretches to get started:

- **Cat-cow stretch:** This gentle flow stimulates the
  spinal nerves, enhancing vagal tone through rhythmic
  movement and breath coordination. Go down onto all
  fours (on hands and knees, arms fully extended), arch
  your back upward, and bend your head downward.
  Then, slowly pull your gut and spine downward as
  you raise your head upward. Repeat 10 to 16 cycles.

- **Child's pose:** This pose encourages diaphragmatic breathing and helps calm the nervous system. From cat-cow, still kneeling on all fours, extend and stretch your arms fully forward, and sit back on your heels. Hold for 30 seconds.

- **Cobra:** Lie face downward, legs fully extended to the rear, and place your hands next to your shoulders. Push upward to raise your head, shoulders, and chest. Extend upward as far as is comfortable, feeling the stretch in your lower back, but don't strain. Hold for 20 to 30 seconds.

- **Downward-facing dog:** From the cobra position, raise your hips toward the ceiling, straighten your legs, and work your hands back until you are in an inverted "V" position. Feel the stretch in your hamstrings and shoulders. Hold for 20 to 30 seconds.

- **Legs up the wall:** Lie on your back with your hips close to a wall. Swing your legs upward to rest against the wall. By elevating the legs, blood flow is directed toward the heart, promoting relaxation and reducing anxiety. Hold for 30 seconds.

Yoga's Benefits on Mental Clarity

Practicing yoga regularly helps improve mental clarity by reducing stress and enhancing focus. Yoga involves mindful movement combined with breath control, which promotes a parasympathetic response and reduces cortisol levels (Ross & Thomas, 2010). This can result in better cognitive function and emotional balance.

Simple Routines for All Levels

- **Beginner's flow:** Start with a gentle 10-minute routine involving the five beginner's poses (see above). Gradually incorporate more poses as your comfort level grows by following short, guided YouTube yoga videos. Be sure to focus on deep breathing and relaxation to ensure proper technique and maximize the benefits.
- **Consistency over intensity:** Practice at least three times a week to maintain the benefits of enhanced vagal tone. Consider performing a 10- to 15-minute yoga stretching routine every morning just after awakening as a great way to start the day.

Stretching and Flexibility Practices

Releasing Muscle Tension for Vagal Tone

Chronic muscle tension can contribute to a heightened state of stress, making it difficult for the body to engage the parasympathetic response. Stretching helps release built-up muscle tension and promotes blood flow, which supports nervous system regulation and enhances vagal activity. Engaging in stretching exercises allows the body to relax, promoting a sense of calm and aiding in stress management (Weerapong et al., 2013).

Stretching Sequences for Relaxation

Incorporating simple stretching sequences into your daily routine can greatly benefit vagal tone and overall relaxation. Here are some effective stretches:

- **Neck stretches:** Slowly tilt your head toward each shoulder to stretch the neck muscles, releasing tension stored in the upper body.
- **Seated forward fold:** Sit on the floor with your legs extended and gently reach toward your toes. This stretch engages the lower back and hamstrings and promotes deep breathing.
- **Chest opener:** Stand or sit with your hands clasped behind your back, gently pulling the shoulders back. This helps open the chest and encourages deeper breaths, stimulating the vagus nerve.

How to Create a Stretching Routine

- **Warm-up first:** Start with light movements such as arm circles or gentle walking to prepare the muscles for stretching.
- **Hold stretches for 20–30 seconds:** Allow each muscle group to relax and extend during each stretch to achieve maximum benefit.
- **Incorporate deep breathing:** Pair each stretch with deep, slow breathing to further stimulate the vagus nerve.
- **Cool down:** Finish with a brief, relaxing pose, such as the child's pose or a supine twist, to help the body transition to a state of calm.

Breath-Centric Exercises

Breath-centric exercises, such as tai chi, Pilates, and other mindful movement practices, play an essential role in enhancing the connection between breath and body, supporting overall nervous system balance, and improving vagal tone. This section will discuss how these forms of movement contribute to the health of the vagus nerve, foundational exercises, and the integration of breathwork into various routines for optimal mind-body harmony.

Tai Chi and Mindful Movement

How Tai Chi Enhances Mind–Body Connection

Tai chi is an ancient Chinese martial art that emphasizes slow, deliberate movements combined with deep, focused breathing. This practice engages both the mind and body, promoting a meditative state that supports mental clarity and reduces stress. Tai chi enhances proprioception (awareness of body position) and promotes a mindful connection to each movement, which contributes to a balanced and harmonious state of being (Wayne & Kaptchuk, 2008).

The practice of tai chi activates the parasympathetic nervous system, helping to lower heart rate and reduce cortisol levels. This activation encourages the release of neurotransmitters like serotonin, which can improve mood and foster a sense of calm. The rhythmic and repetitive nature of tai chi movements is particularly effective for stimulating the vagus nerve, leading to enhanced vagal tone and improved autonomic regulation (Yang et al., 2015).

Vagus Nerve Benefits of Slow, Controlled Movements

Tai chi helps activate the vagus nerve with its emphasis on slow, controlled movements and deep breathing. This activation promotes what we've often referred to as the "rest and digest" state, improving the body's ability to recover from stress and enhancing overall well-being. By engaging in these movements, practitioners can improve HRV, an indicator of a healthy nervous system and good vagal tone (Zou et al., 2018).

Guided Beginners' Tai Chi Sequences

- **Commencement movement:** Start in a standing position with feet shoulder-width apart, and arms relaxed by the sides. Slowly raise your arms in front of you as you inhale deeply. Exhale while gently lowering your arms.
- **Wave hands like clouds:** Shift your weight from one foot to the other while moving your arms in a flowing, cloud-like motion. Maintain deep, rhythmic breathing throughout the sequence.
- **Repulse the monkey:** Step backward while moving one arm forward and the other backward, synchronizing the movement with deep inhalation and exhalation.

Study these and other fundamental tai chi movements by viewing YouTube online instructional training videos. Incorporate these movements into a 10–15 minute daily practice to promote relaxation and enhance vagal tone.

Pilates, Resistance Training, and Core Strength

Core Exercises and Their Impact on Vagal Tone

Pilates and resistance training focus on building core strength, which is essential for posture, stability, and overall physical health. Strong core muscles support diaphragmatic breathing, which stimulates the vagus nerve and promotes the activation of the parasympathetic response. Engaging the core during exercise encourages deeper, more controlled breathing, which enhances the vagal tone and supports nervous system balance (Caldwell et al., 2011).

Breathing Focus in Pilates and Resistance Training for Nervous System Balance

Pilates, in particular, emphasizes the connection between breath and movement. Each exercise is synchronized with specific breathing patterns that maximize the engagement of the core muscles and promote relaxation. This breathing focus helps practitioners remain present and mindful, contributing to reduced stress and better nervous system regulation. Resistance training can similarly incorporate focused breathing, where deep inhalation supports muscle engagement and slow exhalation helps control movement and maintain balance.

Simple Pilates Exercises for Beginners

- **The hundred:** Lie on your back with your legs raised to a tabletop position. Extend your arms alongside your body and lift your head, neck, and shoulders off the mat. Pump your arms up and down while inhaling for 5-second counts and exhaling for 5-second counts, repeating until reaching 100 counts.
- **Roll-up:** Lie flat with arms extended overhead. Slowly roll up one vertebra at a time, reaching for your toes while exhaling. Inhale as you roll back down, engaging your core muscles throughout.
- **Leg circles:** Lie on your back with one leg extended toward the ceiling. Make small, controlled circles with this elevated leg, inhaling for the first half and exhaling for the second half of each circle. Repeat 10 to 12 circles, then repeat with the other leg.

- **Foundational movements:** Incorporate core-strengthening exercises like push-ups, squats, crunches, planks, rowing movements, pull-ups, and overhead presses. These are known as bodyweight resistance exercises and may be performed without equipment or needing a gym membership. As with the other forms of exercise, there are easily accessible online YouTube instructional videos. Pair these movements with focused breathing for maximum engagement and nervous system balance.

Combining Breathwork With Movement

Integrating Breathing Techniques Into Exercise

Integrating breathwork into physical activity can amplify the benefits of both practices. Conscious breathing enhances oxygenation, reduces tension, and activates the vagus nerve, leading to improved focus and relaxation during workouts (Jerath et al., 2006). Whether performing tai chi, Pilates, or resistance exercises, pairing deep, diaphragmatic breathing with movement ensures that the body and mind remain synchronized. Refer back to Chapter 3 to review the breathing exercises if needed.

Benefits of Deep Breathing During Workouts

Deep breathing helps regulate the nervous system, fostering a balance between the sympathetic and parasympathetic states. During workouts, deep breathing not only enhances endurance and performance but also stimulates the vagus nerve to help maintain a state of calm and focus (Laborde et al., 2018). This practice promotes better oxygen flow and reduces muscle fatigue, supporting quicker recovery and sustained energy levels.

Sample Routines for Mind–Body Harmony

- **Warm-up routine:** Start with five minutes of gentle stretching while practicing deep, slow breathing. Incorporate movements like neck rolls and side stretches to release tension and prepare the body for more intense activity.
- **Breath-focused circuit:**
- **Tai chi movements:** Begin with a sequence of "Wave Hands Like Clouds" for two minutes, focusing on deep inhalations and exhalations.
- **Core work:** Perform a set of Pilates "The Hundred" with synchronized breathing for core activation.
- **Resistance exercise:** Incorporate push-ups or squats with a focus on deep inhalation during the lowering phase and slow exhalation as you push up or rise.
- **Cooldown:** Conclude with gentle stretches and seated breathing exercises. Sit cross-legged and place one hand on your abdomen to practice diaphragmatic breathing for five minutes. This cooldown helps reset the nervous system and enhance the vagal tone.

Creating a Sustainable Movement Practice

Sustaining a regular movement practice is essential for maintaining good health, enhancing vagal tone, and fostering mental well-being. However, consistency can be challenging without the right approach. This section focuses on setting realistic fitness goals, maintaining consistency, and tracking progress to create a sustainable and rewarding exercise routine.

Setting Realistic Fitness Goals

Avoiding Burnout With Achievable Goals

Setting realistic goals is crucial to preventing burnout and maintaining a sustainable movement practice. Unrealistic expectations can lead to frustration, discouragement, and, ultimately, abandonment of the routine. Starting with small, achievable goals allows for gradual progress and helps build confidence. Research has shown that setting specific, measurable, and attainable fitness objectives can improve adherence to exercise programs (Locke & Latham, 2002).

To avoid burnout:

- **Begin with manageable sessions:** Start with 15–30 minutes of exercise, focusing on gentle activities like walking, yoga, or Pilates.
- **Incrementally increase intensity:** Once the initial routine feels comfortable, gradually add more challenging elements, such as resistance training or longer sessions.
- **Listen to your body:** Rest and recovery are as essential as the exercise itself; your muscles, ligaments, and joints need time to recover and rebuild. Ensure that your routine includes days for lighter activity or complete rest to prevent overtraining and injury.

Strategies to Make Fitness Enjoyable

Enjoyment is a powerful motivator that can turn exercise into a long-term habit. Here are some strategies to make fitness more enjoyable:

- **Incorporate activities you love:** Whether it's dancing, cycling, or tai chi, choosing activities that you genuinely enjoy will make you more likely to stick with them.
- **Variety is key:** Rotating different types of workouts can prevent boredom and keep your routine interesting. Variation also contributes to reducing repeat activity injuries and wearout.
- **Social support:** Exercising with friends or joining a class can make the experience more enjoyable and add an element of accountability, as well as the benefits of social interaction (Cerin et al., 2017).

Goal-Setting for Mental Well-Being

Setting goals that focus on mental health rather than solely on physical outcomes can enhance motivation and improve well-being. For instance, aiming to reduce stress, improve mood, or enhance focus through movement can shift the emphasis from aesthetics to holistic health. Goals such as "practice mindfulness during workouts" or "incorporate breathwork in stretching" can make your routine more fulfilling and supportive of mental well-being.

Maintaining Consistency

Habits That Support a Lasting Movement Routine

Building consistency in a movement practice requires forming habits that support long-term adherence. Creating a routine that fits seamlessly into your lifestyle makes it easier to commit to daily movement. Here are some tips for fostering consistency:

- **Set a specific time:** Designate a time of day for exercise and treat it as an unmissable appointment. Whether it's a morning yoga session or an evening walk, consistency in timing can reinforce the habit. Do not let yourself make excuses, like "I'll get to it later." Exercise as planned. This will avert feelings of shame for missing a workout.
- **Prepare in advance:** Lay out your workout clothes and any necessary equipment the night before to reduce the mental barriers to starting your routine.
- **Start with mini-routines:** Begin with a short, five-minute stretch or a quick walk to ease into the practice. Over time, this can naturally evolve into longer sessions.

Overcoming Barriers to Daily Exercise

Even with the best intentions, obstacles can arise. Common barriers include time constraints, lack of motivation, or fatigue. To overcome these challenges:

- **Be flexible:** Adapt your routine based on your mood and energy levels. On days when you feel tired, opt for a gentle stretching session or a restorative yoga practice instead of skipping movement entirely.

- **Plan for setbacks:** Anticipate days when your schedule is busier than usual and plan shorter workouts that you can fit in, such as a quick 10-minute walk.
- **Use motivational triggers:** Create reminders or visual cues, such as a calendar with daily check marks or motivational notes, to keep yourself on track (Rhodes et al., 2010).

Adapting Routines Based on Mood and Energy

Adapting your routine to match your energy levels can help maintain consistency without pushing yourself to the point of exhaustion. For example:

- **Low-energy days:** Choose low-impact activities like tai chi, light yoga, gentle stretching, or walking.
- **High-energy days:** Engage in more vigorous activities, such as resistance training, a dance workout, or a full yoga session.

This adaptive approach can prevent burnout and ensure that your movement practice remains a source of well-being rather than stress.

Tracking Progress and Celebrating Wins

Journaling to Track Physical and Mental Benefits

Keeping a journal to document your physical and mental progress is an effective way to stay motivated. Writing down your daily activities, how you felt before and after the workout, and any notable improvements in mood or energy levels can provide valuable insights and reinforce the positive impact of your routine (Pennebaker & Chung, 2011).

Reflection on Mental Health Improvements

Regularly reflecting on how movement affects your mental health can deepen your understanding of its benefits. Journaling about reduced anxiety, better sleep, or improved focus helps highlight the connection between physical activity and emotional well-being. For instance, after a yoga session, you might note feeling more relaxed and clear-headed, which can serve as motivation for future practice.

Celebrating Small Victories for Continued Motivation

Celebrating progress, no matter how small, can boost motivation and make your movement practice more rewarding. Recognizing achievements like completing a week of consistent exercise or learning a new yoga pose can create positive reinforcement. Here's how to celebrate these wins:

- **Reward yourself:** Treat yourself to a new workout playlist, a relaxing bath, or a healthy snack after a milestone, an exceptionally good workout, or reaching a personal best in an activity.
- **Acknowledge progress:** Share your accomplishments with friends or support groups for added encouragement. (But don't brag and risk annoying others.)
- **Visualize success:** Reflect on how far you've come since you started, and visualize the long-term benefits of staying active.

Chapter 5 Summary

Chapter 5 outlines the importance of integrating gentle, breath-centric movement practices to enhance vagal tone, support nervous system health, and foster a sustainable exercise routine that promotes overall well-being.

- **Gentle physical activity for a thriving nervous system:**
  - Daily walks can stimulate vagal tone, boost mood with serotonin, and reduce stress.
  - Outdoor walking promotes relaxation and lowers cortisol levels.
  - Tips include setting a routine, starting with short walks, and incorporating mindfulness.
- **The benefits of yoga for vagal tone:**
  - Yoga positions, such as the child's pose and legs up the wall, activate the vagus nerve.
  - Enhances mental clarity and reduces stress through controlled breathing and movement.
  - Simple yoga routines suitable for all skill levels are beneficial for consistent practice.
- **Stretching and flexibility practices:**
  - Releasing muscle tension through stretching supports vagal tone and relaxation.
  - Specific stretching sequences include neck stretches and seated forward folds.
  - Creating a stretching routine involves warm-ups, 20- to 30-second holds, and deep breathing.
- **Breath-centric exercises:**
  - Tai chi and mindful movement enhance mind-body connection and vagal tone.

- o Pilates and resistance training improve core strength and involve breath-focused exercises.
- o Combining breathing techniques with movement can boost oxygenation and mental focus.
- **Creating a sustainable movement practice:**
  - o Set realistic goals to avoid burnout and make fitness enjoyable.
  - o Maintain consistency with supportive habits and adapt routines based on energy levels.
  - o Track progress through journaling, reflect on mental health benefits, and celebrate small wins for motivation.

Next, more ways to go from fight or flight to rest and digest. "Chapter 6: Parasympathetic Healing Practices for Vagus Nerve Activation" will show you how to access your body's organic reset button for proactive calming effects.

PARASYMPATHETIC HEALING PRACTICES FOR VAGUS NERVE ACTIVATION

Your body's organic "reset" button is more accessible than you might think. With this gift, we must be consistent and trust in its inherent value.

Deep Relaxation Techniques

Deep relaxation techniques are essential for activating the parasympathetic nervous system and enhancing vagal tone, which helps reduce stress and promote mental clarity. Incorporating practices such as guided meditation, visualization exercises, and PMR can significantly improve overall well-being. This section provides an overview of how these techniques contribute to vagus nerve activation, with practical guidance for their integration into daily life.

Guided Meditation for Stress Relief

How Guided Meditation Boosts Vagal Tone

Guided meditation is a powerful tool for stress relief that enhances vagal tone by promoting relaxation and stimulating the parasympathetic nervous system. This practice involves listening to a recorded or live guide who provides step-by-step instructions to help the listener achieve a deep state of calm.

By focusing the mind and encouraging deep breathing, guided meditation lowers heart rate and activates the vagus nerve, improving HRV (Garland et al., 2015).

The benefits of guided meditation extend beyond immediate relaxation. Regular practice can decrease cortisol levels, improve mood, and enhance the body's ability to respond to stress. These benefits make guided meditation an effective practice for managing anxiety, reducing feelings of shame, managing the symptoms of PTSD, and maintaining emotional resilience.

Examples of Meditations for Anxiety

Guided meditations specifically tailored for anxiety often focus on grounding and breath awareness. Examples include:

- **Body scan meditation:** Guides listeners to focus on different parts of the body, releasing tension and promoting awareness.
- **Mindfulness of breath:** Instructs participants to focus solely on the rhythm of their breath, gently redirecting attention to the breath when the mind wanders.

- **Loving-kindness meditation:** Encourages sending kind thoughts to oneself and others, promoting compassion and reducing anxiety (Hofmann et al., 2011).

Apps and Resources for Beginners

Numerous apps and resources offer guided meditations, making it easy for beginners to start their practice. Popular options include:

- **Headspace:** Offers guided meditations focused on stress relief, sleep, and mindfulness.
- **Calm:** Provides meditations tailored to different goals, including anxiety reduction and improved focus.
- **Insight Timer:** Features thousands of free meditations from various instructors, allowing users to choose sessions that best suit their needs.

Visualization Exercises

Mental Imagery for Calming the Nervous System

Visualization exercises, or guided imagery, are relaxation techniques that involve creating mental images to evoke a peaceful state of mind. This practice engages the parasympathetic nervous system by promoting deep relaxation and reducing stress. Visualization can be particularly effective for calming the nervous system because it encourages the brain to produce calming neurotransmitters, enhancing vagal tone and supporting mental well-being (Stefano et al., 2011).

Visualization exercises help shift the body from the "fight or flight" response to the "rest and digest" state, making them valuable for managing stress and anxiety. The use of mental imagery to transport oneself to a serene environment, such as a beach or forest, can help decrease physiological stress markers and improve overall mood.

Step-by-Step for Effective Visualization

- **Find a quiet space:** Sit or lie down in a comfortable position in a quiet environment.
- **Close your eyes:** Take a few deep breaths to center yourself and relax your body.
- **Choose your imagery:** Picture a calming scene, such as a peaceful beach, a meadow filled with flowers, or a quiet forest path.
- **Engage your senses:** Imagine the sensory details of your chosen scene. Feel the warmth of the sun, hear the rustle of leaves, and smell the fresh air.
- **Stay present:** Spend 5–10 minutes immersing yourself in this imagery, maintaining slow, deep breaths.
- **Return slowly:** When ready, open your eyes and bring your attention back to the present, feeling refreshed and relaxed.
- Practical Examples for Daily Use
- **Morning visualization:** Start your day with a brief visualization of a calming scene to set a peaceful tone.
- **Midday reset:** Use a five-minute visualization break during stressful moments to regain focus and lower stress.

- **Bedtime wind-down:** Visualize relaxing scenes before bedtime to promote better sleep and reduce nighttime anxiety.

Progressive Muscle Relaxation

Reducing Tension by Targeting Muscle Groups

As we learned earlier, PMR is a technique that involves tensing and then releasing different muscle groups in the body to promote deep relaxation. This practice helps reduce muscle tension and enhances vagal tone by encouraging a state of relaxation and activating the parasympathetic nervous system. PMR has been shown to decrease stress levels, improve sleep quality, and boost mental clarity (McCallie et al., 2006).

PMR works by teaching the body to recognize the difference between tension and relaxation. By practicing this regularly, individuals can learn to release tension and respond to stress with a calm, controlled reaction.

Benefits for Vagal Tone and Mental Clarity

PMR contributes to improved vagal tone by promoting consistent deep breathing during the practice. The combination of muscle relaxation and slow, diaphragmatic breathing helps signal the brain to engage the parasympathetic response. This practice lowers heart rate and enhances HRV, contributing to greater mental clarity and emotional regulation.

Instructions for a Full-Body Relaxation Session

- **Find a comfortable position:** Sit or lie down in a quiet space with minimal distractions. You may close your eyes for better concentration if desired.

- **Start with deep breaths:** Take a few deep breaths, focusing on a slow inhale and a prolonged exhale.
- **Tense muscle groups:** Starting from your feet, tense the muscles for 5–7 seconds. Focus on the feeling of tension.
- **Release:** Exhale slowly while releasing the tension, and notice the sensation of relaxation.
- **Move up the body:** Progress to the calves, thighs, abdomen, chest, arms, and face, repeating the process of tensing and releasing.
- **End with deep breaths:** Conclude the session with a few more deep breaths, maintaining a relaxed state for a few moments before resuming activities.

PMR can be practiced for 10–20 minutes at any time of day, making it a versatile addition to your routine.

Vocal Toning and Humming

The human voice is a powerful tool for activating the vagus nerve and promoting the "rest and digest" response of the parasympathetic nervous system. Techniques such as humming, chanting, and sound healing can stimulate vagal tone, reduce anxiety and shame, and support overall well-being. This section explores how these practices work and provides practical tips for incorporating them into daily routines.

Humming to Activate the Vagus Nerve

How Vocal Vibrations Stimulate the Vagus Nerve

The vagus nerve runs from the brainstem through the neck and into the chest and abdomen, playing a vital role in regulating various bodily functions, including heart rate and digestion. Humming creates gentle vibrations in the throat that can stimulate the vagus nerve and trigger parasympathetic activity. This activation leads to a cascade of physiological responses, such as slowed heart rate and lowered blood pressure, which promote relaxation and reduce stress (Porges, 2017).

Humming also promotes deeper, diaphragmatic breathing, which enhances oxygen flow and supports the body's ability to engage the parasympathetic response. The resulting state of calm can alleviate symptoms of anxiety, shame, and PTSD and improve gut health, as the vagus nerve is closely linked to the digestive system (Breit et al., 2018).

Simple Humming Exercises to Practice

- **Basic humming practice:**
  - Sit in a comfortable position and close your eyes.
  - Take a deep breath in through your nose.
  - Exhale slowly while humming, focusing on the vibration in your throat and chest.
  - Repeat this process for 5–10 minutes to stimulate the vagus nerve.
- **Humming with breath retention:**
  - Inhale deeply through your nostrils and hold your breath for 4–8 seconds.
  - Exhale slowly while humming. You may find it works better by exhaling through your nostrils.

- Pause for a brief moment before the next inhale.
- Continue for a few minutes, emphasizing long, gentle exhalations.

Benefits for Anxiety and Shame Relief and Gut Health

Regular humming practice can help reduce stress and anxiety by activating the parasympathetic nervous system and promoting a state of relaxation. The stimulation of the vagus nerve improves gut motility and supports healthy digestion, which is particularly beneficial for individuals with stress-related digestive issues (Breit et al., 2018). Additionally, the rhythmic, soothing nature of humming can serve as a form of meditation, further calming the mind and enhancing mental clarity.

Chanting and Singing

Role of Chanting in Calming the Mind

Chanting has been used for centuries in various spiritual and wellness practices to cultivate inner peace and promote mental clarity. The repetitive nature of chanting and the sound vibrations it produces help synchronize the mind and body, enhancing focus and reducing stress. Chanting specific syllables produces vibrations that can stimulate the vagus nerve, fostering a sense of calm and well-being (Kalyani et al., 2011).

The positive effects of chanting extend beyond mental relaxation. Studies show that it can increase HRV, a key indicator of good vagal tone, and improve overall autonomic nervous system function (Kalyani et al., 2011). This response supports resilience to stress and enhances emotional regulation.

Specific Sounds and Chants for Vagal Tone

Certain sounds are particularly effective for stimulating the vagus nerve and promoting relaxation:

- **"Om":** The vibration produced by chanting "Om" resonates throughout the body and can stimulate the vagus nerve, aiding in stress reduction.
- **"Aum":** A variation of "Om" that incorporates a longer sound and more pronounced vibration.
- **Mantras:** Short, repetitive chants such as "So Hum" (meaning "I am that") or "Shanti" (meaning "peace") can be used to focus the mind and activate the vagus nerve. "Om" is often taught as the mantra sound uttered during transcendental meditation.

Practical Tips for Incorporating Chanting Into Your Routine

- **Morning practice:** Start your day with five minutes of chanting to set a calm and focused tone for the day.
- **End-of-day ritual:** Use chanting in the evening as a way to unwind and transition into a restful state.
- **Combine with breathwork:** Pair chanting with deep, controlled breathing to maximize the benefits for the vagus nerve and overall relaxation.

Sound Healing Techniques

Science of Sound Therapy for Mental Health

Sound therapy harnesses the healing properties of sound vibrations to promote mental and physical well-being. It operates on the principle that specific sound frequencies can affect brain-wave patterns, enhancing relaxation and activating the parasympathetic nervous system. Studies have shown that sound therapy can help reduce symptoms of anxiety, lower cortisol levels, and increase feelings of peace and connectedness (Leubner & Hinterberger, 2017).

Vibrational sound therapy can include the use of instruments like singing bowls, tuning forks, and gongs, which create resonant frequencies that help stimulate the vagus nerve and foster a state of deep relaxation. The auditory stimulation provided by these instruments can shift the nervous system from the "fight or flight" mode to "rest and digest," supporting recovery and emotional balance (Bartel et al., 2013).

Tools and Apps for Sound Healing

For those new to sound healing, various tools and apps can help you get started:

- **Singing bowls:** Tibetan singing bowls can be used to produce deep, resonant sounds that promote relaxation.
- **Tuning forks:** Tuning forks set to specific frequencies can be used to target different areas of the body and stimulate the vagus nerve.
- **Apps:** Apps such as **Breethe.com** and **InsightTimer.com** offer sound therapy tracks and guided sessions to help users integrate sound healing into their daily routines.

Short Daily Practices for Vagus Nerve Activation

- **5-minute sound bath:** Sit in a comfortable position, close your eyes, and play a singing bowl or sound healing track. Focus on the vibrations and allow them to wash over you, engaging in deep, steady breathing.
- **Tuning fork practice:** Strike a tuning fork and place it near your ear or on specific pressure points like the chest to promote relaxation.
- **Gong meditation:** Listen to a gong soundtrack while lying down to experience a full-body auditory stimulation that activates the parasympathetic nervous system.

Gentle Cold Exposure

Cold exposure is an accessible and effective practice for stimulating the vagus nerve, promoting parasympathetic activation, and improving overall well-being. Gentle cold exposure methods, such as cold showers, cold compresses, and outdoor cold therapy, can help enhance mental alertness, reduce stress and feelings of shame, alleviate the symptoms of PTSD, and boost energy levels. This section outlines how these practices work, their benefits, and practical steps for safe integration into your routine.

Cold Showers and Their Benefits

Effects of Cold Exposure on the Vagus Nerve

Cold exposure triggers the body's adaptive mechanisms by stimulating the vagus nerve. When the body is exposed to cold temperatures, receptors in the skin send signals to the brain that activate the parasympathetic nervous system. This response encourages the release of neurotransmitters such as norepinephrine and endorphins, which enhance mood, reduce stress, and improve mental focus (van Marken Lichtenbelt et al., 2016). Regular cold exposure can increase vagal tone, which is associated with better HRV and improved resilience to stress (Tipton et al., 2017).

Techniques for Beginners to Start Cold Showers

Starting with cold showers can be intimidating, but gradual exposure can make the practice manageable and effective. Here's how beginners can get started:

- **Start warm and finish cold**: Begin your shower with warm water and gradually lower the temperature over the last 30–60 seconds. Increase the duration of the cold segment over time as your body adapts.
- **Controlled breathing:** Focus on deep, controlled breathing as the cold water flows over your body. This helps manage the initial shock and engages the parasympathetic response.
- **Target specific areas:** Start by exposing the hands, feet, and face to cold water before gradually transitioning to a full-body cold shower.

Benefits for Energy and Mental Alertness

Cold showers are known to enhance energy and mental alertness by stimulating blood circulation and increasing oxygen uptake. The immediate response to cold exposure triggers the release of adrenaline, which can create a sensation of heightened awareness and energy. This practice can also reduce inflammation and promote recovery after physical activity, making it a valuable addition to a holistic wellness routine (Kellogg, 2018).

Cold Compresses and Facial Immersion

Using Cold Compresses for Vagal Tone

Applying cold compresses to the face or neck is a targeted way to stimulate the vagus nerve and activate the parasympathetic response. The cold triggers a reflex known as the mammalian dive response, which slows the heart rate and promotes a state of calm (Panneton, 2013). This technique can be especially helpful for those experiencing acute stress or anxiety. It may be preferable for those who are not up to the cold shower.

Instructions for Safe Face Immersion

Cold facial immersion involves submerging the face in cold water to stimulate the vagus nerve and induce a calming effect. Follow these steps for safe practice:

- **Fill a bowl or sink with cold water:** Fill a large bowl, basin, or bathroom sink with cold water. Adding ice cubes can enhance the temperature but isn't necessary for beginners.
- **Take a deep breath:** Before submerging your face, take a deep, calming breath.
- **Submerge your face:** Lower your face into the water for 10–15 seconds, holding your breath. Ensure your forehead, cheeks, and eyes are submerged.
- **Rest and repeat:** Lift your face out of the water, take a few breaths, and repeat up to three times.

This practice can effectively lower heart rate, reduce stress, and promote relaxation. It's important to listen to your body and avoid submerging for too long, especially if you feel discomfort.

Effects on Heart Rate and Stress Levels

Cold facial immersion activates the vagus nerve through the trigeminal nerve pathway, leading to a decrease in heart rate and an increase in HRV. This reaction can help the body transition from a state of stress to one of relaxation, enhancing emotional resilience and promoting a calm mental state (Breit et al., 2018). The reduction in stress levels can also aid in better digestion and improved gut health, as the vagus nerve plays a significant role in the gut-brain connection.

Outdoor Cold Therapy Techniques

Using Seasonal Changes for Natural Cold Exposure

Seasonal changes provide a natural opportunity for gentle cold exposure, particularly if you live in colder climates. Outdoor activities such as brisk walking or hiking in cool or cold weather can stimulate the vagus nerve without the need for specialized equipment. The body's adaptation to cooler temperatures enhances metabolic efficiency and boosts circulation, leading to increased vagal tone (van Marken Lichtenbelt et al., 2016).

Cold-Weather Breathing Techniques

When engaging in outdoor cold exposure, combining it with specific breathing techniques can help manage the initial shock and promote relaxation:

- **Deep diaphragmatic breathing:** Breathe deeply through your nose and expand your diaphragm, holding for a few seconds before exhaling slowly. This technique helps stabilize your body's response to cold.

- **Box breathing:** Inhale for a count of four, hold for four, exhale for four, and pause for four before repeating. Box breathing helps maintain calm and regulate the body's response to the cold environment.

Safe Practices for Outdoor Exposure

To ensure safety during outdoor cold therapy:

- **Dress in layers:** Wear breathable layers that can be adjusted to maintain comfort while still allowing exposure to the cold.
- **Limit exposure time:** Start with short periods of outdoor cold exposure, such as 5–10 minutes, and gradually increase as your tolerance improves.
- **Stay active:** Keep moving to generate body heat and maintain circulation. Simple exercises like squats, jumping jacks, jump rope, or arm circles can help prevent chills.
- **Hydrate and warm up:** After completing your outdoor exposure, drink warm fluids and perform light stretches to help your body transition back to a warmer state.

Chapter 6 Summary

Chapter 6 outlines practical and effective parasympathetic healing practices to activate the vagus nerve, promote relaxation, and enhance overall mental and physical well-being.

- **Deep relaxation techniques:**
  - Guided meditation boosts vagal tone, reduces stress, and enhances relaxation.
  - Body scan and breath-focused meditations can be highly effective.
  - Consider apps and resources such as Headspace and Calm.
- **Visualization exercises:**
  - Uses mental imagery to calm the nervous system and engage the parasympathetic response.
  - Step-by-step guide for effective visualization practices.
  - Practical applications for morning, midday, and bedtime relaxation.
- **Progressive Muscle Relaxation:**
  - Targets muscle groups to reduce tension and activate the vagus nerve.
  - Benefits include improved mental clarity and better stress management.
  - Follow instructions for a full-body PMR session.
- **Vocal toning and humming:**
  - Humming stimulates vagal tone through vocal vibrations, aiding in anxiety relief and gut health.
- Chanting and singing promote calm, with specific mantra sounds like "Om" being particularly effective.
  - Tips for incorporating vocal practices into daily routines and the use of sound healing tools.
- **Gentle cold exposure:**
  - Cold showers stimulate the vagus nerve, enhance energy, and improve mental alertness.
  - Cold compresses and facial Immersion offer targeted vagal stimulation and stress reduction.

- Outdoor cold therapy safely uses natural cold exposure and combines it with breathing techniques.

Moving on. "Chapter 7: Mindset Shifts for Moments of Inner Peace" will help you to dismiss diminishing or negative thoughts and redirect your mind to achieve a state of inner peace and calm.

7

MINDSET SHIFTS FOR MOMENTS OF INNER PEACE

True wellness is found within: You alone have the capacity to observe and gently work with all kinds of agonizing or destructive thoughts and mental images to achieve a state of higher vibration or being.

Embracing a Compassionate, Growth Mindset

Developing a mindset that fosters inner peace requires adopting new ways of thinking and acting that break cycles of stress and self-doubt. Embracing a compassionate, growth-oriented mindset can lead to enhanced well-being, improved resilience, and a healthier response to life's challenges. This section explores how to break free from self-doubt, practice gratitude, and build resilience through self-care.

Breaking Free From Self-Doubt

Recognizing and Reframing Limiting Beliefs

Self-doubt is often rooted in limiting beliefs—internalized ideas that restrict personal growth and potential. These beliefs, such as "I am not good enough" or "I will fail," can become self-fulfilling prophecies if left unchallenged. The first step in overcoming self-doubt is recognizing these beliefs and reframing them in a way that aligns with a more positive, growth-focused mindset. For example, replace "I am not capable" with "I am learning and growing every day."

Reframing limiting beliefs involves:

- **Self-awareness:** Identify recurring negative thoughts and analyze their origins.
- **Reframing:** Counter negative thoughts with balanced and constructive affirmations.
- **Practice:** Regularly remind yourself of your rephrased beliefs through journaling or affirmations.

Vagus Nerve's Role in Stress and Mindset

The vagus nerve plays a critical role in how the body responds to stress and influences your mindset. When the vagal tone is low, the body remains in a state of heightened alertness, making it difficult to adopt a positive perspective. Enhancing vagal tone through practices such as deep breathing, meditation, and vocal toning can help shift the nervous system from the sympathetic "fight or flight" state to the parasympathetic "rest and digest" state, facilitating a calmer mindset (Breit et al., 2018).

Steps to Cultivate Self-Compassion

Self-compassion involves treating oneself with kindness during times of failure or difficulty rather than engaging in harsh self-criticism. This practice can improve emotional resilience and support a positive, growth-oriented mindset. Here's how to develop self-compassion:

- **Acknowledge your humanity:** Recognize that making mistakes is part of being human. Replace self-judgment with understanding.
- **Practice mindful self-talk:** Use phrases like "I am doing my best" or "I am worthy of love and support" to reinforce compassionate thoughts.
- **Forgive yourself:** Let go of past mistakes and view them as opportunities for learning and growth.

Practicing Gratitude

Benefits of Gratitude on Mental Health

Gratitude has been shown to increase happiness, improve mental health, and boost overall well-being. When practiced regularly, gratitude can enhance vagal tone, reduce stress, and foster positive emotions (Emmons & Stern, 2013). The act of focusing on what is good in life helps shift the mind away from negative thoughts and promotes a sense of abundance and contentment.

To reinforce gratitude in daily life, create affirmations and post them in visible places such as a bathroom mirror, fridge, or work desk. Examples of affirmations include:

- "I am grateful for the opportunities that come my way."
- "Each day is a gift, and I choose to see the positive."
- "I am thankful for the support and love in my life."

Simple Daily Gratitude Exercises

Starting a gratitude journal is one of the most effective ways to make gratitude a daily habit. Take a few minutes each day to write down three things you are grateful for. These can range from major life events to simple pleasures, such as a warm cup of tea or a sunny day. The act of journaling opens your mind to appreciate even the simple things, reinforces positive thinking, and helps build a habit of appreciation.

Integrating Gratitude Into Routine

Integrating gratitude into your daily routine doesn't have to be time-consuming. Here are simple ways to weave gratitude into your life:

- **Morning gratitude:** Before you begin your day, think of one thing you're thankful for and say it out loud. For example, being grateful for the blessing of sleep and the ability to awaken.
- **Evening reflection:** Before going to sleep, say out loud three things you are grateful for. This practice can help create a sense of peace and set the stage for restful sleep.
- **Mindful moments:** During the day, take short breaks to pause and reflect on something positive. This could be as simple as appreciating a kind word from a friend or a moment of quiet. Even a bird flying by and chirping or a child's laughter.

Building Resilience Through Self-Care

Developing Self-Care Rituals

Self-care is vital for building resilience and maintaining emotional balance. Regular self-care practices, such as exercise, creative hobbies, and social connections, help boost energy levels and improve vagal tone. Exercise, in particular, is known to enhance mental well-being and raise energy vibration by releasing endorphins and supporting nervous system health (Ratey & Hagerman, 2008).

Mindset Practices for Resilience: Stoicism

Developing a resilient mindset involves more than just positive thinking; it requires engaging in practices that build inner strength and adaptability. Facing fears and stepping out of one's comfort zone is a powerful way to build resilience and courage. Taking small "leaps of faith," such as pursuing a new skill or speaking up in a meeting, can foster confidence and reveal a deeper understanding of your true self. You may have to make an effort to force yourself to action, but it's worth it.

Stoic philosophy offers valuable insights for cultivating resilience. Stoicism teaches that while we cannot control external events, we can control our reactions to them. Practicing Stoic techniques, such as focusing on what you can control and accepting what you cannot, helps build a mindset that is less affected by stress and setbacks (Pigliucci, 2017).

Examples of Resilient Thinking

- **Reframe challenges as opportunities:**
  Instead of viewing obstacles as failures, see them as

chances for growth and learning. Tell yourself, "I've got this."

- **Practice voluntary discomfort:** Occasionally engage in activities that are outside your comfort zone to build mental toughness. For example, taking a cold shower or fasting for a day can help develop resilience and self-discipline.
- **Adopt a long-term perspective:** Remind yourself that most difficulties are temporary and that you have the strength to overcome them.

Mindfulness as a Daily Practice

Mindfulness is a powerful practice that involves maintaining awareness of the present moment with an attitude of acceptance and non-judgment. Cultivating mindfulness can foster self-awareness, reduce stress, and build resilience. Integrating mindfulness into daily routines can transform how you respond to challenges and maintain emotional balance. This section explores techniques for mindful awareness, developing a meditation habit, and employing stress reduction practices.

Mindful Awareness of Thoughts

Observing Without Judgment

One of the core aspects of mindfulness is learning to observe your thoughts without judgment. This means noticing your thoughts as they arise and acknowledging them without labeling them as "good" or "bad." This approach encourages acceptance and allows you to sit with emotions, even those that may feel uncomfortable. Accepting that "it's okay to not feel okay" can be profoundly liberating and help reduce the tendency to react impulsively to negative thoughts.

To practice this, try a simple mindfulness exercise:

- **Set a timer:** Find a quiet space and set a timer for 5–10 minutes.
- **Sit comfortably:** Close your eyes and take a few deep breaths.
- **Observe:** Notice any thoughts that come to mind. Rather than engaging with them or pushing them away, observe them like clouds passing in the sky.
- **Label lightly:** If needed, you can label thoughts (e.g., "worrying" or "planning") and then return to your breath.

Mindfulness Techniques for Beginners

Beginners often benefit from guided practices that help culti- vate mindful awareness. Techniques include:

- **Body scan:** Bring attention to different parts of your body, starting from your toes and working upward. Notice any tension or sensations without attempting to change them.
- **5-4-3-2-1 technique:** Identify five things you can see, four you can touch, three you can hear, two you can smell, and one you can taste. This exercise grounds you in the present moment and enhances awareness.

Benefits of Self-Awareness and How to Begin Cultivating It

Mindful awareness fosters self-reflection and helps you respond to stress more effectively. By observing thoughts without judgment, you create a space between stimulus and response, which can lead to healthier reactions (Kabat-Zinn, 2013). To cultivate mindfulness daily:

- **Incorporate mini-breaks:** Take short breaks during your day to pause and observe your breathing.
- **Mindful moments:** Bring awareness to routine activities such as washing dishes or walking by focusing on the sensations and movements involved. Take note while you are eating to be aware of each spoonful and how you chew and swallow.
- **Reflective journaling:** Spend a few minutes at the end of the day journaling about what thoughts you observed and how you responded to them. These can be brief notations or longer descriptions if you prefer.

Developing a Meditation Habit

How Meditation Strengthens Resilience

Meditation is a key practice that helps build resilience by strengthening the mind's ability to remain focused and calm under pressure. Regular meditation trains the brain to handle stress more effectively and promotes emotional regulation by enhancing the function of the prefrontal cortex, the area responsible for decision-making and self-control (Tang et al., 2015). Meditation also supports vagal tone, which helps maintain a balanced nervous system and improves stress response (Gerritsen & Band, 2018).

(We covered meditation in Chapter 3 if you'd like to refer back for more instruction.)

Starting Small and Building Consistency

Beginners should start with short, manageable meditation sessions and gradually increase their duration as comfort and familiarity grow. Here's how to start:

- **Set realistic goals:** Begin with 2–5 minutes per day and slowly extend to 10–15 minutes over time.
- **Anchor your practice:** Meditate at the same time each day, such as first thing in the morning or before bedtime, to build consistency.
- **Be patient:** It's normal for the mind to wander. When this happens, gently redirect your attention back to your breath or chosen focus point.

Making Meditation a Daily Routine

Many people have tried to meditate, but did not continue after a few sessions. This behavior traces to several common setbacks:

- They became bored. It's normal to find it tedious sitting still, eyes closed, trying to keep a clear, thoughtless, mind for 20 minutes.
- Thoughts and images keep trying to intrude, and the person becomes frustrated, and feels the meditation is not working.
- Sessions are missed or put off due to scheduling conflicts, or simply forgetting to pause to meditate.

These setbacks can be avoided, with trust in the effectiveness of regular practice. It's important to make meditation a habit; this can be done by assigning a time that will be free and uninterrupted every day. For example, before breakfast, lunch, or dinner. Some find meditating before going to bed beneficial in relaxing for the night and getting better sleep each night.

Gently ignore incoming, unwanted thoughts, without getting annoyed. Just let the thoughts go and refocus on breathing and the humming or a mantra.

Meditation can be brief, even just a few minutes. An increasingly popular form of meditation, Kirtan Kriya, is known as the "12-minute miracle" due to its brevity and positive mental and physical benefits (Alzheimer's Research & Prevention Foundation, 2024).

Regular meditation can create long-lasting changes in how you perceive stress, improving resilience and emotional balance.

Stress Reduction Techniques

Simple Practices for Real-Time Stress Relief

Integrating mindfulness with stress reduction techniques can provide immediate relief when stress levels rise. Popular methods derived from dialectical behavior therapy (DBT), cognitive behavioral therapy (CBT), and acceptance and commitment therapy (ACT) can be effective:

- **DBT's "TIPP" strategy:** TIPP stands for Temperature, Intense exercise, Paced breathing, and Progressive muscle relaxation. For example, splashing cold water on your face can trigger the dive response and activate the vagus nerve to calm the body

(Linehan, 2015). Refer back to Chapter 6, Section 3, for detailed instructions on cold showers and cold water therapy.

- **CBT's thought reframing:** When faced with stress, identify negative thought patterns and replace them with more balanced, realistic thoughts. For instance, shift "I can't handle this" to "I've faced challenges before, and I can manage this one."
- **ACT's acceptance techniques:** Accept difficult emotions as they arise and commit to actions aligned with your values instead of fighting or avoiding the feelings.

Mindful Breathing Under Pressure

Breathwork can be an invaluable tool for stress management. Deep, diaphragmatic breathing activates the parasympathetic nervous system, reduces cortisol levels, and promotes relaxation (Jerath et al., 2006). Simple breathing techniques include:

- **Box breathing:** Inhale for 4 counts, hold for 4 counts, exhale for 4 counts, and hold for another 4 counts. Repeat this cycle for 2–3 minutes to reset your stress response. You may recall the instructions for box breathing in Chapter 3.
- **4-7-8 breathing:** Inhale for 4 counts, hold for 7 counts, and exhale for 8 counts. This technique helps slow the heart rate and promotes a sense of calm. This is similar to box breathing, with slight variations in the counts, and no holding the breath after the exhale; just pause for a second and then resume the inhale count.

Positive Visualization Strategies

Visualization is a mindfulness tool that uses mental imagery to create a sense of calm and focus. By envisioning positive outcomes or peaceful scenes, you can help manage stress and foster resilience. We covered visualization techniques in Chapter 3; here are two summaries of techniques you can use:

- **Calm place visualization:** Close your eyes and imagine a place where you feel safe and relaxed, such as a beach or forest. Engage all your senses to make the image vivid. Ignore the thoughts that may intrude by refocusing on the image.
- **Outcome visualization:** Visualize yourself successfully managing a stressful situation, feeling confident and in control. This can help build self-assurance and reduce anxiety about upcoming events.

Tools for Emotional Regulation

Emotional regulation is essential for mental health and well-being. Developing tools for managing emotions can help maintain balance, resilience, and a positive outlook. This section explores the benefits of journaling for self-reflection, techniques for setting boundaries, and practices for self-compassion —all crucial strategies for regulating emotions and enhancing vagal tone.

Journaling for Self-Reflection

Benefits of Writing Down or Recording Thoughts for Mental Clarity

Journaling is a simple yet powerful tool for fostering self-awareness and mental clarity. Writing down thoughts allows individuals to process their emotions, understand patterns in their thinking, and gain perspective. Research indicates that expressive writing can help reduce stress and improve mental health by allowing people to confront and organize their thoughts (Pennebaker & Chung, 2011). Journaling engages the brain's cognitive and emotional processing centers, promoting a deeper understanding of oneself and aiding in emotional regulation, especially if the entries you write are carefully considered and thoughtful. We initially covered journaling in Chapter 5; here are some further directions for effective practice.

Prompts for Emotional Exploration

To get started with reflective journaling, use prompts that encourage deeper exploration of emotions:

- **"What emotions** did I feel today, and what triggered them?"
- **"What am I proud of** accomplishing today?"
- **"How did I handle stress,** and what could I have done differently?"
- **"What thoughts** have been occupying my mind, and how do they serve me?"

These prompts can help unpack complex emotions and reveal underlying patterns in thought processes. By consistently practicing self-reflection, you can develop greater self-awareness and emotional intelligence.

Consistent Journaling Practices

For journaling to be effective, consistency is key:

- **Set a regular schedule:** Dedicate 10–15 minutes daily or a few times a week to journaling.
- **Choose a comfortable method:** Whether you prefer writing in a notebook or typing on a digital device, choose the format that feels most natural. Some studies indicate handwritten entries have more cognitive benefits than digital data entry, but it's really just a matter of preference.
- **Be honest and non-judgmental:** Write openly without censoring your thoughts. The process is meant for self-exploration, not perfection.

Journaling not only enhances mental clarity but also improves emotional balance and resilience, aiding in the development of a stronger vagal tone and overall well-being.

Setting Boundaries for Mental Health

Recognizing Stress Triggers and What to Do About It

Setting boundaries is crucial for managing stress and maintaining mental health. In order to establish effective boundaries, it's essential to recognize stress triggers—situations or behaviors that lead to discomfort or emotional exhaustion. These can include excessive demands at work, overcommitment to social obligations, or interactions with people who drain energy. It's important to know when it's time to say "No."

Steps to Recognize and Manage Stress Triggers:

- **Reflect on your day:** Identify moments that caused significant stress or emotional discomfort.
- **Write them down:** Recording triggers in a journal can help you become more aware of recurring patterns.
- **Plan a response:** Develop strategies for handling triggers, such as politely declining additional responsibilities or taking breaks during overwhelming tasks.

Techniques for Healthy Boundary-Setting With Yourself and Others

Boundary setting requires assertiveness and clarity. Techniques for establishing boundaries include:

- **Communicate clearly:** Use "I" statements to express your needs, such as "I need some time alone after work to recharge."
- **Be consistent:** Reinforce boundaries consistently so others understand and respect them.
- **Practice saying no:** Learn to refuse additional tasks or engagements that strain your time and energy without feeling guilty.

Standing up for yourself is essential for maintaining mental, physical, and emotional health. When you enforce boundaries, you create space for self-care and personal growth, which positively impacts vagal tone and reduces stress (Smith et al., 2008).

Benefits of Boundaries on Vagal Tone

Personal boundaries help maintain a balanced nervous system by reducing chronic stress. When individuals set and enforce healthy boundaries, they experience less emotional burnout and heightened feelings of control and safety. This sense of safety activates the parasympathetic nervous system, which supports vagal tone and promotes relaxation.

Practicing Self-Compassion

Treating Oneself With Kindness and Nurturing Self-Respect

Self-compassion is about treating oneself with the same kindness and care that one would offer a close friend. It involves recognizing that everyone makes mistakes and faces challenges, and it is okay to extend understanding to oneself during difficult times. Practicing self-compassion helps replace negative self-talk with more nurturing, positive language, fostering emotional resilience and well-being (Neff, 2011). It may not be apparent to you, but your subconscious mind is listening and taking note of positive thoughts.

How to Manage Chronic Self-Criticism and Replace It With Encouragement

Chronic self-criticism can erode self-esteem and contribute to feelings of inadequacy. To combat this, try the following strategies:

- **Identify self-critical thoughts:** Pay attention to moments when self-critical thoughts arise and note them in a journal. You will be able to note these criticisms with practice.

- **Challenge these thoughts:** Ask yourself if the thoughts are true or if you are being overly harsh. Do not try to "beat yourself up," but instead, give yourself a break; take it easy on what you've done or are thinking.
- **Reframe with positive language:** Replace negative statements like "I always mess up" with constructive ones such as "I'm learning and growing, and mistakes are part of that process."

Over time, self-compassion can shift your inner dialogue from one of criticism to one of support, enhancing both self-esteem and interpersonal relationships. This practice not only boosts emotional well-being but also makes individuals more inclined to treat others with kindness and respect. These acts of kindness will be reciprocated for further benefits.

Impact on Overall Well-Being

The practice of self-compassion has been linked to increased emotional resilience and greater life satisfaction. When people treat themselves kindly, they are better equipped to handle challenges without becoming overwhelmed. This internal support system also reduces cortisol levels and improves the body's ability to manage stress (Neff & Germer, 2012).

Practicing self-compassion benefits not just the individual but also those around them. Self-compassionate individuals are more patient and empathetic, fostering healthier, more supportive relationships. The positive reinforcement that comes from self-compassion strengthens confidence and can lead to a cycle of positivity that enhances overall mental health.

Chapter 7 Summary

Chapter 7 emphasizes the importance of nurturing a positive mindset, practicing gratitude, and developing emotional regulation tools to foster inner peace and resilience.

- **Embracing a compassionate, growth mindset:**
  - Break free from self-doubt by recognizing and reframing limiting beliefs.
  - Understand the vagus nerve's role in stress and mindset, and practice self-compassion to enhance resilience.
  - Develop self-compassion through mindful self-talk and forgiveness.
- **Practicing gratitude:**
  - Gratitude improves mental health, enhances vagal tone, and fosters positive emotions.
  - Use affirmations and gratitude journals to incorporate gratitude into daily life.
  - Simple practices like saying three things you're grateful for before bed can make a significant impact.
- **Building resilience through self-care:**
  - Create self-care rituals, including exercise and activities that raise energy levels.
  - Adopt resilient thinking by stepping out of your comfort zone and learning from challenges.
  - Apply Stoic principles to focus on what you can control, disregard what you can't, and develop mental toughness.

- **Mindfulness as a daily practice:**
  - Observe thoughts without judgment and practice self-awareness with mindfulness techniques.
  - Develop a consistent meditation habit to strengthen resilience and emotional balance.
  - Use stress-reduction techniques like mindful breathing and positive visualization for real-time relief.
- **Tools for emotional regulation:**
  - Journaling promotes mental clarity and helps with emotional exploration.
  - Set boundaries to manage stress, improve mental health, and support vagal tone.
  - Practice self-compassion to replace self-criticism with encouragement, boosting self-esteem and overall well-being.

You've completed most of the journey now, with one chapter to go. "Chapter 8: Carving out Your Lifelong Body-Mind-Spirit Wellness Journey" wraps up the step-by-step changes that will empower your personal transformation through vagus nerve management and toning.

CARVING OUT YOUR LIFELONG BODY-MIND-SPIRIT WELLNESS JOURNEY

Slow, small steps create epic change: Continue to empower your mind, body, and overall life force on an everyday basis.

Developing a Personalized Wellness Plan

A lifelong wellness journey requires intentional planning, consistent effort, and adaptability. In order to sustain mind–body–spirit harmony, it's essential to create a personalized plan that prioritizes your mental and physical health, integrates achievable daily routines, and tracks progress for long-term growth. This section explores how to identify key priorities, design a balanced routine, and reflect on your program to maintain motivation and alignment with your wellness goals.

Identifying Key Priorities

Assessing Areas of Focus for Mental and Physical Health

Wellness is multidimensional, encompassing physical, mental, and emotional health. Start by assessing the areas of your life that need attention. Reflect on questions such as:

- Overall, how do I feel on a scale of 1 to 10?
- How is stress affecting my body and mind?
- Do I feel energized or fatigued throughout the day?
- What aspects of my mental or physical health do I want to improve?

By evaluating your current state, you can pinpoint priorities, whether it's managing anxiety, improving digestive health, or enhancing resilience.

Tools for Identifying Personal Wellness Goals

Several tools and exercises can help clarify wellness goals:

- **Wellness wheel:** Use a wellness wheel to assess key areas such as physical health, emotional balance, relationships, and personal growth. "A wellness wheel describes the integration of eight important dimensions of wellness: emotional, financial, environmental, intellectual, occupational, physical, social and spiritual" (*Wellness Wheel Assessment,* 2024). Learn more by using the search term "wellness wheel" to identify which segments need the most attention.
- **SMART goals:** Create goals that are Specific, Measurable, Achievable, Relevant, and Time-bound.

For example: Practice breath-focused meditation for 10 minutes daily to improve vagal tone and reduce stress, and practice yoga stretches and poses every day before breakfast.

- **Journaling:** Reflective journaling, as explained in the previous chapter, can reveal patterns, such as triggers for anxiety or moments of joy, helping you understand where to focus your efforts.

Importance of Individualized Planning

Wellness is not one-size-fits-all. An individualized plan accounts for your unique needs, preferences, and lifestyle. Personalizing your wellness journey ensures that the changes you implement are meaningful and sustainable. For example, if vigorous exercise feels overwhelming, start with gentle activities like yoga or walking.

Creating a Balanced Daily Routine

Sample Routines for Mental and Digestive Health

A balanced daily routine can improve mental clarity, support digestive health, and strengthen vagal tone. Here's an example of a wellness-focused daily routine:

- **Morning:**
  - Practice gratitude by writing down three things you're grateful for. Try to select different sources of gratitude each day, which forces you to be reflective. Refer to Chapter 6 for more about gratitude and its benefits.
  - Engage in a 5–10-minute diaphragmatic breathing exercise to start the day calmly. For

example, box breathing or 4-7-8 breathing, which we covered in Chapter 3.

- Eat a nutrient-rich breakfast, such as a smoothie with leafy greens, chia seeds, and berries for gut health. Or a bowl of oat-based muesli with fresh or dried fruit and a few spoonfuls of low-fat oat or almond-based yogurt.

- **Afternoon:**
  - Take a 10–15 minute walk after lunch to enhance digestion and vagal tone.
  - Integrate a brief mindfulness practice, such as body scanning or 5 minutes of focused breathing, to reduce mid-day stress.

- **Evening:**
  - Engage in gentle stretches or a restorative yoga session. Do this before dinner or before going to bed.
  - Reflect on the day in your journal, noting progress, challenges, and areas for gratitude.

Integrating Small Changes for Big Results

Wellness transformation doesn't require drastic changes. Small, consistent actions can accumulate and yield significant long-term benefits. For example:

- Replace processed snacks with whole, gut-friendly foods like nuts and fresh or dried fruit.
- Dedicate 5–10 minutes daily to meditation, gradually increasing the duration.
- Focus on one new habit at a time, such as improving sleep hygiene by limiting screen time before bed and

ensuring good restorative sleep for eight hours each night, going to sleep, and awakening at the same time each night.

Tips for Adapting Routines to Life's Demands

Life's unpredictability requires flexibility in wellness routines:

- **Simplify on busy days:** When time is limited, opt for quick practices like 2 minutes of mindful breathing or a short walk. When possible, take several short walks and take part in breathing sessions.
- **Embrace imperfection:** Missing a day doesn't mean failure. Resume your practice the next day without guilt.
- **Adjust as needed:** Reassess your goals periodically and adapt routines to align with new priorities or challenges.

Tracking Your Progress and Reflecting

Measuring Improvements in Vagal Tone and Wellness

Tracking progress is vital to sustaining motivation and celebrating growth. Improvements in vagal tone, mental health, and physical well-being can be measured through:

- **Heart rate variability:** Use a fitness tracker or app to monitor HRV as an indicator of vagal tone. HRV is the fine-tuned variations in the timing of each heartbeat and is an indicator of cardiovascular health.
- **Mood and energy levels:** Keep a log of daily

energy levels, mood stability, and stress responses. Notice patterns over time.

- **Health indicators:** Track digestive health, sleep quality, and physical endurance to identify positive changes. These may not be things you tend to think about, but once you become aware, you can recognize and monitor changes.

Journaling and Reflecting for Motivation

Journaling is an invaluable tool for reflection and growth. Documenting your journey can do the following:

- Highlight successes and reinforce positive habits.
- Provide insight into setbacks and strategies to overcome them.
- Encourage gratitude by focusing on what's working well.

Use prompts to guide your journaling, such as:

- "What accomplishments—large and small—did I achieve today?"
- "What challenges did I face, and how did I respond?"
- "How have I grown since starting my wellness journey?"

Celebrating Milestones to Reinforce Habits

Acknowledging milestones, no matter how small, creates a sense of accomplishment and strengthens commitment. Examples of milestones include:

- Complete a week of daily meditation.
- Notice improved sleep patterns.
- Achieve a personal goal, such as a 30-day streak of journaling or consistent exercise.

Ways to celebrate milestones:

- Treat yourself to something rewarding, like a relaxing bath, a new book, or a healthy meal at your favorite restaurant. Or buy yourself a small gift.
- Share achievements with friends or a supportive community to boost encouragement. A supportive community can be formed by several people who share common interests in self-improvement.
- Reflect on your progress by comparing where you started to where you are now.

Sustainable Self-Care Habits

Sustainable self-care habits are the foundation of long-term physical, mental, and emotional well-being. Building and maintaining these habits can help foster balance, resilience, and fulfillment. This section explores daily practices for sustainable wellness, strategies for staying motivated and consistent, and the value of celebrating even the little steps of personal progress.

Daily Practices for Long-Term Balance

Small but Impactful Daily Habits

Small, consistent habits can have a cumulative effect on wellness over time. These manageable practices are more likely to become ingrained in your routine, leading to lasting change. Examples of impactful habits include:

- Start the day with five minutes of mindful breathing or gratitude journaling.
- Drink a glass of water first thing in the morning to hydrate the body and kick start metabolism.
- Take short breaks to stretch or move during the workday to reduce tension and boost energy.
- Be careful not to sit too often or too long. Movement is beneficial, while sitting too much all day and evening may negate exercise workouts earlier in the day.

Consistency in these small habits fosters a ripple effect, improving mental clarity, physical health, and emotional balance.

Incorporating Breathwork, Movement, and Diet

A holistic approach to self-care involves attention to breathwork, movement, and nutrition:

- **Breathwork:** Practices like diaphragmatic breathing and the physiological sigh can activate the vagus nerve, reduce stress, and improve focus (Jerath et al., 2006). Aim for 5–10 minutes of focused breathwork daily.
- **Movement:** Incorporating even gentle activity, such as walking or yoga, supports nervous system health and releases "feel good" endorphins. Strive for 30 minutes of active movement most days.
- **Diet:** A balanced, nutrient-dense diet rich in fiber, healthy fats, and anti-inflammatory foods nourishes

both body and mind. Plan meals with whole, unprocessed ingredients to sustain energy and gut health.

Look up the Mediterranean diet and follow its practices of vegetables, fruits, whole grains, nuts and seeds, cold water fish like salmon, eggs, low-fat oat or almond milk, and extra virgin olive oil.

Example Day-to-Day Wellness Routines

- **•Morning:**
  - Hydrate with water and engage in five minutes of gratitude journaling.
  - Practice 10 minutes of breath-focused meditation or gentle stretching.
  - Eat a nourishing breakfast, such as oatmeal topped with nuts and fruit, plus oat or almond-based yogurt.
  - Have several organic, free-range eggs each week. This can be one egg each day or two eggs every other day.
- **Afternoon:**
  - Take a brisk walk after lunch to enhance digestion and mental clarity.
  - Include a mindful snack, like fresh veggies or a handful of seeds.
- **Evening:**
  - Reflect on the day's accomplishments and challenges in a journal.
  - Wind down with restorative yoga or deep breathing before bed.

o Avoid caffeine in coffee and strong tea close to
   bedtime, and don't consume alcohol late in the
   evening; it can mess with sleep cycles.

Keeping Motivated and Consistent

Strategies to Maintain Momentum

Staying motivated is essential for making self-care habits
sustainable. Motivation prevents boredom and burnout. Here
are strategies to keep you on track:

- **Set clear intentions:** Focus on why each habit
  matters to your overall well-being. For example,
  regular breathwork reduces stress and improves focus.
- **Visualize the outcome:** Imagine how consistent
  self-care will benefit you, such as better sleep,
  improved mood, or enhanced energy.
- **Reward yourself:** Celebrate adherence to habits
  with small, meaningful recognitions, like a daily log of
  progress. Maybe you can treat yourself to a little extra
  dessert at dinner.

Overcoming Barriers to Routine

Challenges are inevitable, but planning for obstacles can help
you stay consistent:

- **Time constraints:** Break self-care practices into
  smaller segments. If you can't commit to a 30-minute
  workout, try a 10-minute walk or stretching session, or
  as noted, a couple of very brief walks or yoga
  stretches. You can achieve a full day's fitness quota by

breaking the exercises into short segments: It all adds up!

- **Lack of motivation:** Use accountability partners or apps to keep yourself engaged. Sharing your goals with a friend can add encouragement.
- **Negative thinking:** Reframe setbacks as opportunities to learn and grow. For instance, if you skip a practice, reflect on what caused the interruption and how to adjust.

Using Habit Tracking to Stay on Course

Tracking habits can reinforce consistency and help you visualize progress. Tools for habit tracking include:

- **Journals:** Use a physical or digital journal to log daily self-care activities and their effects. Review the sections on journals in Chapters 5 and 7.
- **Apps:** Apps like Habitica, Streaks, or HabitBull gamify habit tracking, making it fun and engaging.
- **Checklists:** Simple checklists or habit grids can provide a satisfying sense of completion when you mark off completed tasks.

Reviewing your progress periodically can boost motivation by showing how far you've come.

Celebrating Small Personal Achievements

Importance of Acknowledging Progress

Recognizing progress, no matter how small, reinforces positive habits and builds confidence. Achieving milestones—such as meditating daily for a week or choosing healthy meals consistently—serves as motivation to keep going. Celebrating small wins keeps you engaged and focused on your long-term goals.

Ways to acknowledge progress include:

- Share achievements with a supportive community or loved ones.
- Reflect on the positive changes in your journal.
- Treat yourself to a small, non-food reward, like a yoga, tai chi, or fitness class.

Self-Compassion for Setbacks

No journey is without obstacles, and self-compassion is critical when setbacks occur. Instead of viewing a missed practice as a failure, see it as part of the process. Acknowledge your efforts and remind yourself that consistency, not perfection, drives success (Neff & Germer, 2013).

To practice self-compassion:

- Speak kindly to yourself, using phrases like "It's okay to have off days; I'll try again tomorrow."
- Reflect on challenges without judgment and identify solutions for moving forward.
- Use setbacks as learning experiences to adjust routines or identify additional support.

Reinforcing Healthy Patterns

Sustaining self-care habits requires intentional reinforcement. Build momentum by celebrating successes and staying connected to the benefits of your practices. For example:

- Reflect on how breathwork has improved your stress response.
- Notice how regular movement has increased your energy and mood.
- Acknowledge the mental clarity and resilience gained through consistent journaling.

Each positive experience reinforces the value of self-care and strengthens your commitment to sustaining it.

Integrating Social Support and Community

Building and nurturing social connections is essential for long-term well-being. A strong community can provide emotional support, encouragement, and accountability, all of which contribute to a balanced body–mind–spirit connection. This section explores the benefits of finding supportive networks, sharing your journey, and using your experience to help others.

Finding Supportive Connections

Benefits of a Like-Minded Community

Connecting with individuals who share similar values and goals fosters a sense of belonging and mutual encouragement. A like-minded community provides a safe space to share experiences, exchange ideas, and learn from others' journeys. Research has shown that strong social connections contribute to lower stress levels, improved mental health, and increased longevity (Holt-Lunstad et al., 2010).

Supportive communities also help strengthen resilience by offering empathy and understanding during challenging times. Knowing you're not alone can provide comfort and inspire continued growth, making it easier to sustain positive habits and overcome setbacks.

Seeking Social Support for Mental Health

Social support plays a critical role in emotional regulation and mental health. Whether it's confiding in a trusted friend or participating in a support group, having others to lean on can reduce feelings of isolation and foster emotional stability. Conversations with empathetic listeners often lead to new perspectives and insights, enhancing emotional well-being and reducing anxiety.

If you're unsure where to begin, consider these types of support:

- **Close relationships:** Cultivate open communication with family or friends.
- **Peer support:** Join groups that focus on shared challenges or interests, such as fitness classes or mindfulness workshops.
- **Professional support:** Seek guidance from therapists or counselors who can offer specialized advice and techniques for managing stress.

Resources for Finding Support Networks

There are many ways to find supportive communities:

- **Local meetups:** Platforms like Meetup.com can help you connect with groups focused on health, mindfulness, or personal development.
- **Social media groups:** Many online platforms host private or public groups dedicated to wellness topics.

- **Community centers:** Libraries, gyms, and community centers often offer classes or events that foster connection.
- **Volunteering:** Engaging in volunteer activities introduces you to compassionate, service-oriented individuals.

Sharing Your Journey and Progress

Importance of Sharing Experiences

Sharing your personal wellness journey can deepen your sense of purpose and inspire others to embark on their own paths. Being open about your challenges and triumphs fosters authenticity and builds trust, strengthening your relationships. Studies show that shared experiences can improve emotional resilience and create a sense of mutual support (Seppala et al., 2013).

Sharing your progress also reinforces your commitment to personal growth. When you discuss your journey, you remind yourself of the progress you've made and the reasons behind your efforts, which can boost motivation.

How to Inspire Others Through Your Journey

By sharing your story, you demonstrate that wellness is attainable and that challenges are part of the process. To inspire others:

- **Be honest:** Share both your struggles and successes to show that growth involves effort and perseverance.
- **Offer practical tips:** Share specific practices or strategies that have worked for you, such as morning routines or breathwork techniques.

- **Celebrate small wins:** Acknowledge progress in your journey, showing that even minor improvements are significant milestones.

You might inspire others through casual conversations, blog posts, or social media updates. Sharing your wellness practices, such as how meditation or healthy eating transformed your life, can encourage others to take the first step toward their own goals.

Creating Accountability With Friends or Groups

Accountability partners or groups can help you stay consistent and focused on your wellness goals. Sharing your intentions with others creates a sense of responsibility and ensures regular check-ins for progress updates. Consider the following:

- **Form a small group:** Start a group with friends or family to practice yoga, journaling, or other self-care habits together.
- **Schedule regular check-ins:** Plan weekly calls or meetings to discuss progress, challenges, and next steps.
- **Join wellness challenges:** Participate in group challenges focused on fitness, mindfulness, or healthy eating.

Expanding to Help Others

Using Your Knowledge to Be Supportive

Once you've made progress in your wellness journey, consider sharing your knowledge and experiences to help others. Becoming a source of encouragement can strengthen your own practices while creating a ripple effect of positivity. Offering support to someone struggling can improve their sense of hope and motivate you to stay committed to your habits.

Practical ways to support others include:

- **Sharing resources:** Recommend books, apps, or techniques that have been beneficial for you.
- **Listening actively:** Offer a non-judgmental ear to friends or family who need guidance or encouragement. Be compassionate, not critical.
- **Encouraging self-care:** Gently remind others of the importance of prioritizing their health and well-being. Use your own personal examples of what you've done and the positive results.

Volunteering, Mentoring, and Paying It Forward

Volunteering and mentoring are powerful ways to expand your impact. By helping others, you contribute to their growth and well-being while reinforcing your own sense of purpose. Volunteering has also been shown to improve mental health, reduce stress, and foster a sense of community (Jenkinson et al., 2013).

- **Mentoring:** Share your experiences with someone just starting their wellness journey. Offer guidance and accountability as they navigate challenges. But be sensitive by being a coach, not a commander.
- **Volunteering:** Participate in wellness-related initiatives, such as leading a mindfulness class at a community center or assisting with health-focused events. If you are benefitting from exercise, offer to help others to start their own fitness program. Share

your excitement with how good it makes you feel to work out and be physically active.

- **Paying it forward:** Use your knowledge to educate and inspire others, creating a chain reaction of positive change that can spread from person to person and from group to group.

Making a Positive Impact on Others' Wellness Journeys

Helping others often leads to a deeper understanding of your own journey. Supporting someone else requires reflection, empathy, and reinforcement of the lessons you've learned, which further strengthens your practices. Teaching is a highly effective way to learn even complex subjects.

Some ideas for making a positive impact include:

- **Organizing workshops:** Host sessions on mindfulness, breathwork, or fitness to share valuable skills. It may take some time to find an ideal location and to encourage people to join you.
- **Promoting awareness:** Use social media or community platforms to spread awareness about wellness practices. Post announcements on bulletin boards in community centers and supermarkets, for example, to reach out to people.
- **Creating a support network:** Facilitate a space —this can be an online Zoom video conference environment—where individuals from various locations can come together to share their experiences and support one another.

Chapter 8 Summary

Chapter 8 emphasizes a comprehensive approach to wellness by creating personalized strategies, maintaining sustainable habits, and building supportive communities to ensure long-term success and fulfillment.

- **Developing a personalized wellness plan:**
  - Identify key priorities for mental and physical health using tools like wellness wheels and journaling.
  - Design individualized, adaptable daily routines to support mental clarity and digestive health.
  - Track progress through metrics like HRV, journaling, and reflective practices.
- **Sustainable self-care habits:**
  - Incorporate small, impactful daily practices such as mindful breathing, gentle movement, and a nutrient-rich diet.
  - Stay motivated with habit-tracking tools and clear intentions while overcoming barriers with flexibility.
  - Celebrate milestones and practice self-compassion for setbacks to reinforce positive habits.
- **Integrating social support and community:**
  - Build connections with like-minded individuals through local meetups, online groups, or volunteering.
  - Share your wellness journey to inspire others and create accountability within supportive networks.
  - Expand your impact by mentoring, teaching, or

volunteering to promote well-being in others' lives.

Well done! You have completed *Vagus Nerve Brain-Belly Reset* and are equipped to conquer anxiety, stress, shame, and Complex PTSD. The next section is the "Conclusion," followed by "References," a listing of every resource used to inform and enrich the content of this book. Most are accessible online and links are provided.

CONCLUSION: EMBRACING A LIFELONG JOURNEY OF VAGAL HEALTH

Your journey toward enhanced vagus nerve health represents a profound commitment to nurturing your mind, body, and emotions. The vagus nerve, a central player in your parasympathetic nervous system, connects every aspect of your well-being —regulating stress responses, fostering emotional balance, and maintaining digestive and immune health. By caring for this vital nerve, you unlock a gateway to resilience, calm, and vitality.

Throughout this book, you've explored a variety of tools and strategies, from mindful breathwork, exercises, and cold exposure to nourishing dietary choices and supportive relationships. Each practice strengthens your ability to thrive in the face of life's challenges. By prioritizing vagal tone, you've learned how to reduce anxiety, stabilize your gut health, and enhance your overall quality of life. These strategies are not fleeting fixes; they are transformative habits that, when sustained, can lead to lasting wellness.

A Journey Worth Continuing

As you move forward, remember that wellness is a lifelong journey, not a destination. There will be days when your efforts flow effortlessly and others when maintaining consistency feels more challenging. That's okay—progress is never linear. Each small step matters and every act of self-care strengthens the foundation of your health.

Continue to nurture your vagus nerve with the practices that resonate most deeply with you. Whether it's yoga or tai chi before breakfast, taking a daily walk, pausing for a moment of mindfulness, or connecting with loved ones, these simple habits are the threads that weave a tapestry of well-being. When practiced consistently, they create a ripple effect that enhances not only your own health but also the lives of those around you.

Reflect regularly on the progress you've made and the positive changes you've experienced. Use setbacks as opportunities for growth rather than reasons for self-criticism. By doing so, you cultivate not only a balanced nervous system but also a compassionate and resilient mindset.

A Call to Inspire Action

Your wellness journey doesn't end with you—it has the potential to inspire others. Share your experiences, challenges, and successes with your family and community, whether through casual conversations, social media, or support groups. When others see the positive impact these practices have had on your life, they may feel empowered to begin their own journeys.

Consider this book not just as a resource for your personal growth but as a tool to pass on to others. If you've found value in these strategies, please **leave a favorable review** so that others may discover the benefits of vagus nerve health. By doing so, you contribute to a ripple effect of wellness, inspiring more people to embrace holistic practices that support mind-body harmony.

The Path Ahead

The work you've done is meaningful, and the journey ahead is filled with potential. By consistently practicing these strategies and maintaining an open mind, you pave the way for a life of balance, resilience, and joy. The tools you've gained are yours to use, adapt, and share as you navigate the ever-changing rhythms of life.

Remember, wellness is a gift that grows with intention and care. Take what you've learned, put it into action, and let your journey toward lifelong vagal health become an example for others to follow. The power to transform your life—and the lives of those around you—is in your hands.

Kimberley Elisabeth Gray

REFERENCES

Barratt, E. L., & Davis, N. J. (2015, March 26). Autonomous sensory meridian response (ASMR): A flow-like mental state. *PeerJ*, 3, e851. https://doi.org/10.7717/peerj.851

Bartel, L. R., Chen, R., Alain, C., & Ross, B. (2013, April 1). Sound therapy for mental health: Mechanisms and evidence. *Canadian Journal of Psychiatry*, 58(4), 195-203. https://doi.org/10.1177/0706743713058000403

Berman, M. G., Jonides, J., & Kaplan, S. (2009, January 1). The cognitive benefits of interacting with nature. *Research Gate, Psychological Science, 19*(12), 1207-1212. https://www.researchgate.net/publication/23718837_The_Cognitive_Benefits_of_Interacting_With_Nature

Bischoff, S. C. (2011, March 14). 'Gut health': A new objective in medicine? *BMC Medicine, 9*(24). https://doi.org/10.1186/1741-7015-9-24

Bishehsari, F., Magno, E., Swanson, G., Desai, V., Voigt, R. M., & Forsyth, C. B. (2017). Alcohol and gut-derived inflammation. *Alcohol Research: Current Reviews*, 38(2), 163–171. https://www.ncbi.nlm.nih.gov/pmc/articles/PMC5513685/

Block, M. L., & Calderón-Garcidueñas, L. (2009, September). Air pollution: Mechanisms of neuroinflammation and CNS disease. *Trends in Neurosciences*, 32(9), 506-516. https://doi.org/10.1016/j.tins.2009.05.009

Bonaz, B., Bazin, T., & Pellissier, S. (2018, February 6). The vagus nerve at the interface of the microbiota-gut-brain axis. *Frontiers in Neuroscience, 12*, 49. https://doi.org/10.3389/fnins.2018.00049

Breit, S., Kupferberg, A., Rogler, G., & Hasler, G. (2018, March 12). Vagus nerve as modulator of the brain–gut axis in psychiatric and inflammatory disorders. *Frontiers in Psychiatry, 9*, 44. https://doi.org/10.3389/fpsyt.2018.00044

Buckly, G. (2020, April 25). Homeostasis. *Biology Dictionary.* https://biologydictionary.net/homeostasis/

Calder, P. C. (2017, September 12). Omega-3 fatty acids and inflammatory processes: From molecules to man. *Biochemical Society Transactions, 45*(5), 1105-1115. https://doi.org/10.1042/BST20160474

Caldwell, K., Adams, M., Quin, R., & Harrison, M. (2011, July). Pilates, mindfulness and somatic education. *Journal of Bodywork and Movement Therapies, 15*(3), 329-338. https://doi.org/10.1016/j.jbmt.2010.06.003

Camilleri, M. (2019, May 10). Leaky gut: mechanisms, measurement and clin-

ical implications in humans. *National Library of Medicine.* https://pubmed.
ncbi.nlm.nih.gov/31076401/

Carabotti, M., Scirocco, A., Maselli, M. A., & Severi, C. (2015, April-June). The
gut-brain axis: Interactions between enteric microbiota, central and enteric
nervous systems. *Annals of Gastroenterology, 28*(2), 203-209. https://www.
ncbi.nlm.nih.gov/pmc/articles/PMC4367209/

Cerin, E., Leslie, E., Sugiyama, T., & Owen, N. (2009, December). Associations
of multiple physical activity domains with mental well-being. *ScienceDirect.*
https://www.sciencedirect.com/science/article/
abs/pii/S1755296609000283

Chang, A.-M., Aeschbach, D., Duffy, J. F., & Czeisler, C. A. (2014, December
22). Evening use of light-emitting eReaders negatively affects sleep, circadian timing, and next-morning alertness. *Proceedings of the National
Academy of Sciences, 112*(4), 1232-1237. https://doi.org/10.1073/pnas.
1418490112

Chassaing, B., Koren, O., Goodrich, J. K., Poole, A. C., Srinivasan, S., Ley, R. E.,
Gewirtz, A. T. (2015, February 25). Dietary emulsifiers impact the mouse
gut microbiota promoting colitis and metabolic syndrome. *Nature,
519*(7541), 92-96. https://doi.org/10.1038/nature14232

Clapp, M., Aurora, N., Herrera, L., Bhatia, M., Wilen, E., Wakefield, S. (2017,
September 15). Gut microbiota's effect on mental health: The gut-brain
axis. *Clinics and Practice, 7*(4), 987. https://doi.org/10.4081/cp.2017.987

Conrad, A., & Roth, W. T. (2007). Muscle relaxation therapy for anxiety disorders: It works but how? *Journal of Anxiety Disorders, 21*(3), 243-264.
https://doi.org/10.1016/j.janxdis.2006.08.001

Emmons, R. A., Stern, R. (2013, June 17). Gratitude as a psychotherapeutic
intervention. *Journal of Clinical Psychology, 69*(8), 846-855. https://doi.org/
10.1002/jclp.22020

Esch, T., & Stefano, G. B. (2010). The neurobiology of stress management.
Neuro Endocrinology Letters, 31(1), 19–39. https://pubmed.ncbi.nlm.nih.
gov/20150886/

Fülling, C., Dinan, T. G., Cryan, J. F. (2020, March). Gut microbe to brain
signaling: What happens in vagus. *Neuroscience & Biobehavioral Reviews,
97*, 302-314. https://doi.org/10.1016/j.neubiorev.2018.08.014

Gao, Q., Li, P., Li, G., & Lv, X. (2017, July 7). Serotonin and circadian rhythm
in sleep-wake regulation. *Neuropsychiatric Disease and Treatment, 13*,
2039-2048. https://doi.org/10.2147/NDT.S140801

Garland, E. L., Howard, M. O., Zubieta, J. K., & Froeliger, B. (2015,
September). Restructuring reward mechanisms in the brain to treat addiction. *Trends in Cognitive Sciences, 19*(8), 515-524. https://doi.org/10.1016/
j.tics.2015.07.002

Gerritsen, R. J., & Band, G. P. H. (2018, October 18). Breath of life: The respiratory vagal stimulation model of contemplative activity. *Frontiers in Human Neuroscience, 12*, 397. https://doi.org/10.3389/fnhum.2018.00397

Gómez-Pinilla, F. (2008, July). Brain foods: The effects of nutrients on brain function. *Nature Reviews Neuroscience, 9*(7), 568-578. https://doi.org/10.1038/nrn2421

Grossman, P., Niemann, L., Schmidt, S., & Walach, H. (2004, July). Mindfulness-based stress reduction and health benefits: A meta-analysis. *Journal of Psychosomatic Research, 57*(1), 35-43. https://doi.org/10.1016/S0022-3999(03)00573-7

Hartig, T., Mitchell, R., de Vries, S., & Frumkin, H. (2014,January 20). Nature and health. *Annual Review of Public Health, 35*, 207-228. https://doi.org/10.1146/annurev-publhealth-032013-182443

Hewlings, S. J., & Kalman, D. S. (2017, October 22). Curcumin: A review of its effects on human health. *Foods, 6*(10), 92. https://doi.org/10.3390/foods6100092

Hofmann, S. G., Grossman, P., & Hinton, D. E. (2011, November). Loving-kindness and compassion meditation: Potential for psychological interventions. *Clinical Psychology Review, 31*(7), 1126-1132. https://doi.org/10.1016/j.cpr.2011.07.003

Holt-Lunstad, J., Smith, T. B., & Layton, J. B. (2010, July 27). Social relationships and mortality risk: A meta-analytic review. *PLoS Medicine, 7*(7), e1000316. https://journals.plos.org/plosmedicine/article?id=10.1371/journal.pmed.1000316

Huberman, A. (2021, March 8). *Tools for managing stress and anxiety.* [Podcast episode]. *Huberman Lab Podcast.* https://ai.hubermanlab.com/d/6dc057ea-c4f4-11ed-a531-870fa2ab23a0

Jenkinson, C. E., Dickens, A. P., Jones, K., Thompson-Coon, J., Taylor, R., Rogers, M., Bambra, C., Lang, I., & Richards, S. (2013, August 23). Is volunteering a public health intervention? A systematic review and meta-analysis of the health and survival of volunteers. *BMC Public Health, 13*(1), 773. https://doi.org/10.1186/1471-2458-13-773

Jerath, R., Edry, J. W., Barnes, V. A., & Jerath, V. (2006). Physiology of long pranayamic breathing: Neural respiratory elements may provide a mechanism that explains how slow deep breathing shifts the autonomic nervous system. *Medical Hypotheses, 67*(3), 566-571. https://doi.org/10.1016/j.mehy.2006.02.042

Jia, S. S., Wardak, S., Raeside, R., & Partridge, S. R. (2022). The impacts of junk food on health. *Frontiers for Young Minds, 10*. https://doi.org/10.3389/frym.2022.694523

Kabat-Zinn, J. (2013). *Full Catastrophe Living: Using the Wisdom of Your Body and Mind to Face Stress, Pain, and Illness. New York: Bantam Books.*

Kahn, M., Sheppes, G., & Sadeh, A. (2013). Sleep and emotions: A focus on micro-level sleep processes. *Encyclopedia of Sleep* (Vol. 2, pp. 233-237).

Kalyani, B. G., Venkatasubramanian, G., Arasappa, R., Rao, N. P., Kalmady, S. V., Behere, R. V., & Gangadhar, B. N. (2011, January-June). Neuro Hemodynamic correlates of 'OM' chanting: A pilot functional magnetic resonance imaging study. *International Journal of Yoga, 4*(1), 3-6. https://doi.org/10.4103/0973-6131.78171

Khanna, S., Tosh, P. K., Berg, A. M. (2018, August 1). High fructose intake: Consequences and recommendations. *Nutrition Reviews, 76*(11), 791-799. https://doi.org/10.1093/nutrit/nuy033

Kok, B. E., Fredrickson, B. L. (2010, December). Upward spirals of the heart: Autonomic flexibility, as indexed by vagal tone, reciprocally and prospectively predicts positive emotions and social connectedness. *Biological Psychology, 85*(3), 432-436. https://doi.org/10.1016/j.biopsycho.2010.09.005

Koulivand, P. H., Khaleghi Ghadiri, M., & Gorji, A. (2013, March 14). Lavender and the nervous system. *Evidence-Based Complementary and Alternative Medicine, 2013*, 681304. https://doi.org/10.1155/2013/681304

Laborde, S., Mosley, E., & Thayer, J. F. (2017, February 19). Heart rate variability and cardiac vagal tone in psychophysiological research – Recommendations for experiment planning, data analysis, and data reporting. *Frontiers in Psychology, 8*, 213. https://doi.org/10.3389/fpsyg.2017.00213

Lehrer, P. M., & Gevirtz, R. (2014, July). Heart rate variability biofeedback: How and why does it work? *NIH National Library of Medicine.* https://pubmed.ncbi.nlm.nih.gov/25101026/

Leubner, D., & Hinterberger, T. (2017, July 6). Reviewing the effectiveness of music interventions in treating depression. *Frontiers in Psychology, 8*, 1109. https://doi.org/10.3389/fpsyg.2017.01109

Linehan, M. M. (2015). DBT Skills Training Manual. *Mindsplain.* https://mindsplain.com/wp-content/uploads/2020/09/DBT_handouts.pdf

Locke, E. A., & Latham, G. P. (2002). Building a practically useful theory of goal setting and task motivation. *American Psychologist, 57*(9), 705-717. https://doi.org/10.1037/0003-066X.57.9.705

Lovallo, W. R., Whitsett, T. L., al'Absi, M., Sung, B. H., Vincent, A. S., & Wilson, M. F. (2005, September). Caffeine stimulation of cortisol secretion across the waking hours in relation to caffeine intake levels. *Psychosomatic Medicine, 67*(5), 734-739. https://doi.org/10.1097/01.psy.0000181270.20036.06

Marselle, M. R., Irvine, K. N., & Warber, S. L. (2019, February). Walking for well-being: A qualitative review of the benefits of walking on mental health.

Social Science & Medicine, 56(10), 202-213. https://doi.org/10.1016/j. socscimed.2019.01.039

Mayfield, R. D., Harris, R. A., & Schuckit, M. A. (2008). Genetic factors influencing alcohol dependence. *Neuropsychopharmacology Reviews, 33*(4), 735-750. https://bpspubs.onlinelibrary.wiley.com/doi/full/10.1038/bjp. 2008.88

Mayo Clinic Staff. (2024, August 16). *Post-traumatic stress disorder.* Mayo Clinic.   https://www.mayoclinic.org/diseases-conditions/post-traumatic-stress-disorder/symptoms-causes/syc-20355967

McCallie, M. S., Blum, C. M., & Hood, C. J. (2006, October 4). Progressive muscle relaxation. *Journal of Human Behavior in the Social Environment, 13*(3), 51-66. https://doi.org/10.1300/J137v13n03_04

McEwen, B. S. (2007). Physiology and neurobiology of stress and adaptation: Central role of the brain. *Physiological Reviews, 87*(3), 873-904. https:// pubmed.ncbi.nlm.nih.gov/17615391/

Mischoulon, D., & Freeman, M. P. (2013). Omega-3 fatty acids in psychiatry. *Psychiatric Clinics of North America, 36*(1), 15-23.

Moszeik, E.N., von Oertzen, T., & Renner, K-H. (2020, September 8). Effectiveness of a short Yoga Nidra meditation on stress, sleep, and well-being in a large and diverse sample. *Springer Nature.* https://link.springer. com/article/10.1007/s12144-020-01042-2

Neff, K. D. (2011). *Self-compassion: The proven power of being kind to yourself.* New York: William Morrow.

Neff, K. D., & Germer, C. K. (2012, October 15). A pilot study and randomized controlled trial of the mindful self-compassion program. *Journal of Clinical Psychology, 69*(1), 28-44. https://doi.org/10.1002/jclp.21923

Ouwehand, A. C., Lagström, H., Suomalainen, T., & Salminen, S. J. (2010, August 1). Effect of probiotics on constipation, fecal azoreductase activity, and fecal mucin content. *Microbial Ecology in Health and Disease, 14*(4), 197-204.   https://www.semanticscholar.org/paper/Effect-of-Probiotics-on-Constipation%2C-Fecal-and-in-Ouwehand-Lagstr%C3%B6m/ 5b0408b2d4d7f03104b049b163be37fb82d742b9

Pavlov, V. A., & Tracey, K. J. (2017, January 16). Neural regulation of immunity: Molecular mechanisms and clinical translation. *Nature Neuroscience, 20*(2), 156-166. https://doi.org/10.1038/nn.4477

Pennebaker, J. W., & Chung, C. K. (2011). Expressive writing: Connections to physical and mental health. *Handbook of Health Psychology, 263-284.*) https://psycnet.apa.org/record/2013-01232-018

Pigliucci, M. (2017). *How to be a stoic: Using ancient philosophy to live a modern life.* New York: Basic Books

Poerio, G. L., Blakey, E., Hostler, T. J., & Veltri, T. (2018, June 20). More than a feeling: Autonomous sensory meridian response (ASMR) is characterized by reliable changes in affect and physiology. *PLoS ONE, 13*(6), e0196645. https://doi.org/10.1371/journal.pone.0196645

Popkin, B. M., D'Anci, K. E., & Rosenberg, I. H. (2010, August). Water, hydration, and health. *Nutrition Reviews, 68*(8), 439-458. https://doi.org/10. 1111/j.1753-4887.2010.00304.x

Porges, S. W. (2001, October). The polyvagal theory: Phylogenetic substrates of a social nervous system. *International Journal of Psychophysiology, 42*(2), 123-146. https://doi.org/10.1016/S0167-8760(01)00162-3

Porges, S. W. (2007, February). The polyvagal perspective. *Biological Psychology, 74*(2), 116-143. https://doi.org/10.1016/j.biopsycho.2006. 06.009

Porges, S. W. (2009). Reciprocal influences between body and brain in the perception and expression of affect: A polyvagal perspective. *The Handbook of Emotion Elicitation and Assessment*, 27-45. https://psycnet.apa.org/ record/2009-20446-002

Porges, S. W. (2011). *The polyvagal theory: Neurophysiological foundations of emotions, attachment, communication, and self-regulation.* W W Norton & Co. https://psycnet.apa.org/record/2011-04659-000

Porges, S. W. (2017). *The pocket guide to the polyvagal theory: The transformative power of feeling safe.* New York: W.W. Norton & Company.

Practice the 12 minute yoga meditation exercise. (2024). Alzheimer's Research & Prevention Foundation. https://alzheimersprevention.org/research/kirtan-kriya-yoga-exercise/

Ratey, J., & Hagerman, E. (2008). *Spark: The revolutionary new science of exercise and the brain.* New York: Little, Brown.

Rhodes, R. E., Fiala, B., & Conner, M. (2010, January 16). A review and meta-analysis of affective judgments and physical activity in adult populations. *Annals of Behavioral Medicine, 38*(3), 180-204. https://doi.org/10.1007/ s12160-009-9147-y

Ross, A., & Thomas, S. (2010, January 16). The health benefits of yoga and exercise: A review of comparison studies. *Journal of Alternative and Complementary Medicine, 16*(1), 3-12. https://doi.org/10.1089/acm.2009.0044

Seppala, E. M., Rossomando, T., & Doty, J. R. (2013, Summer). Social connection and compassion: Important predictors of health and well-being. *StanfordMedicine. Social Research: An International Quarterly, 80*(2), 411-430. https://ccare.stanford.edu/article/social-connection-and-compassion-important-predictors-of-health-and-well-being/

Slavin, J. (2013, April 22). Fiber and prebiotics: Mechanisms and health benefits. *Nutrients, 5*(4), 1417-1435. https://doi.org/10.3390/nu5041417

Smith, B. W., Dalen, J., Wiggins, K., Tooley, E., Christopher, P., & Bernard, J. (2008). The brief resilience scale: Assessing the ability to bounce back.

National   Library   of   Medicine.   https://pubmed.ncbi.nlm.nih.gov/
18696313/

Srivastava, J. K., Shankar, E., & Gupta, S. (2010, September 27). Chamomile: A herbal medicine of the past with a bright future. *Molecular Medicine Reports, 3*(6), 895-901. https://doi.org/10.3892/mmr.2010.377

Summer, J., & Peters, B. (2024, February 26). *What is non-sleep deep rest?* Sleep Foundation. https://www.sleepfoundation.org/meditation-for-sleep/what-is-non-sleep-deep-rest

Swanson, D., Block, R., & Mousa, S. A. (2012, January). Omega-3 fatty acids EPA and DHA: Health benefits throughout life. *Advances in Nutrition, 3*(1), 1-7. https://doi.org/10.3945/an.111.000893

Tang, Y.-Y., Holzel, B. K., & Posner, M. I. (2015). The neuroscience of mindfulness meditation. *Nature Reviews Neuroscience, 16*(4), 213-225. https://doi.org/10.1038/nrn3916

Taren, A., Gianaros, P., Greco, C., Lindsay, E., Fairgrieve, A., Brown, K.W., Rosen, R., Ferris, J., Julson, E., Marsland, A., Bursley, J., Ramsburg, J., & Creswell, J.D. (2015, December). Mindfulness meditation training alters stress-related amygdala resting state functional connectivity: A randomized controlled trial. *Social Cognitive and Affective Neuroscience, 10*(12), 1758-1768. https://doi.org/10.1093/scan/nsv066

Telles, S., Singh, N., Kumar, A., & Balkrishna, A. (2013, November 7). Effect of yoga or physical exercise on physical, cognitive and emotional measures. *National LIbrary of Medicine.* https://pubmed.ncbi.nlm.nih.gov/24199742/

Thayer, J. F. & Lane, R. D. (2009, February). Claude Bernard and the heart-brain connection: Further elaboration of a model of neurovisceral integration. *Neuroscience & Biobehavioral Reviews, 33*(2), 81-88. https://doi.org/10.1016/j.neubiorev.2008.08.004

Thayer, J. F. & Lane, R. D. (2000). A model of neurovisceral integration in emotion regulation and dysregulation. *Journal of Affective Disorders, 61*(3), 201-216. https://pubmed.ncbi.nlm.nih.gov/11163422/

Thayer, J. F. & Sternberg, E. M. (2006, December 8). Beyond heart rate variability: Vagal regulation of allostatic systems. *Annals of the New York Academy of Sciences, 1088*(1), 361-372. https://doi.org/10.1196/annals.1366.014

Tracey, K. J. (2009, June). Reflex control of immunity. *Nature Reviews Immunology, 9*(6), 418-428. https://doi.org/10.1038/nri2566

Unno, K., Fujitani, K., Takamori, N., Takabayashi, F., & Okubo, T. (2018, January 1). L-Theanine, a constituent of green tea, inhibits [(3)H]GABA transaminase activity and increases brain serotonin, dopamine, and GABA levels. *Bioscience, Biotechnology, and Biochemistry, 62*(4), 816-817. https://doi.org/10.1271/bbb.62.816

van der Kolk, B. A. (2014). *The body keeps the score: Brain, mind, and body in the healing of trauma*. New York: Viking.

Visioli, F., & Galli, C. (2002, June 3). Biological properties of olive oil phytochemicals. *Critical Reviews in Food Science and Nutrition, 42*(3), 209-221. https://doi.org/10.1080/10408690290825529

Wayne, P. M., & Kaptchuk, T. J. (2008, January-February). Challenges inherent to T'ai Chi research: Part II-defining the intervention and optimal study design. *Journal of Alternative and Complementary Medicine, 14*(2), 191-197. https://doi.org/10.1089/acm.2007.7173

Weerapong, P., Hume, P. A., Kolt, G. S. (2013, July 19). Stretching: Mechanisms and benefits for sport performance and injury prevention. *Physical Therapy Reviews, 9*(4), 189-206. https://doi.org/10.1179/108331904225007078

Wellness wheel assessment. (2024). University of New Hampshire. https://extension.unh.edu/health-well-being/programs/wellness-wheel-assessment

Wielgosz, J., Goldberg, S. B., Kral, T. R. A., Dunne, J. D., & Davidson, R. J. (2019). Mindfulness meditation and psychopathology. *Annual Review of Clinical Psychology, 15*(1), 285–316. https://doi.org/10.1146/annurev-clinpsy-021815-093423

Wright, K., P., McHill, Andrew W., Birks, Brian R., Griffin, Brandon R., Rusterholz, T., & Chinoy, Evan D. (2013). Entrainment of the human circadian clock to the natural light-dark cycle. *Current Biology, 23*(16), 1554–1558. https://doi.org/10.1016/j.cub.2013.06.039

Yang, Y., Verkuil, B., van der Veen, D. C., Brosschot, J. F., & Thayer, J. F. (2015, August). The effects of Tai Chi on stress and wellbeing: A systematic review. *Journal of Psychosomatic Research, 78*(6), 499-510. https://doi.org/10.1016/j.jpsychores.2015.03.008

Young, S. N. (2007, November). How to increase serotonin in the human brain without drugs. *Journal of Psychiatry & Neuroscience, 32*(6), 394-399. https://www.ncbi.nlm.nih.gov/pmc/articles/PMC2077351/

Zope, S.A., & Zope, R.A., (2013, January-June). *Sudarshan kriya yoga: Breathing for health.* International Journal of Yoga. https://pmc.ncbi.nlm.nih.gov/articles/PMC3573542/

Zou, L., Zhang, Y., Yang, L., & Loprinzi, P. D. (2018, May). The benefits of Tai Chi for patients with chronic diseases. *Sports Medicine, 48*(9), 2135-2150. https://pubmed.ncbi.nlm.nih.gov/31072005/

ABOUT THE AUTHOR

Kimberley Elisabeth Gray is a passionate health and wellness advocate dedicated to exploring the healing power of the vagus nerve. This mystical nerve has the potential to support chronic anxiety and depression, optimize gut health, and taps into an indi-  vidualized sense of spiritual well-being for inner peace and mental clarity.

Kim holds a Bachelor's degree in Psychology and additional diplomas in Holistic Nutrition and Functional Strength Training. Drawing from her journey with combating mental illness, drug and alcohol addiction as well as Irritable Bowel Syndrome (IBS), Kimberley has firsthand experience with the transformative potential of mindful vagus nerve engagement.

Upon experiencing a metamorphosis in her health, she began researching how this fascinating nerve can positively influence the intricate connection between the human mind, body and one's personal energy field. Fueled by a mission to make these life-transformative tools accessible, Kimberley shares her insights through her books, offering readers practical tech- niques and evidence-based strategies to support mind-body- spirit health by awakening them to the essence of the Vagus Nerve.

THANK YOU

Thank you kindly for purchasing my book. You had many options, but you decided on this one. I truly hope your mind, body and spirit will thrive as you continue to practise these holistic healing strategies and exercises on a day-today basis.

Before we part ways, I have a small favor to ask. Could you please consider posting a review on the platform? Writing a review is the best and easiest way to support the work of independent authors like myself. Your feedback is essential for me to continue writing books that help people like yourself achieve a more present, harmonized state of being. It would mean a lot to hear from you. Thank you with all my heart!

>>Leave a review on Amazon US <<
>>Leave a review on Amazon UK <<
>>Leave a review on Amazon CA<<

FREE BOOK!

The Nervous System Regulation Workbook

A journey of discovery into how our nervous system works, how it impacts our daily lives and practical skills that can strengthen our resilience to stress.

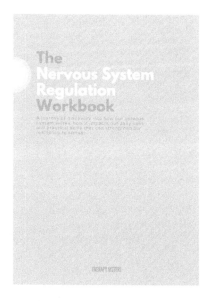

Get your copy now!